# PAUL HOLLYWOOD

## THE BIOGRAPHY

## A S DAGNELL

JOHN BLAKE

Published by John Blake Publishing Ltd,
3 Bramber Court, 2 Bramber Road,
London W14 9PB, England

www.johnblakebooks.com

www.facebook.com/johnblakebooks ⓣ
twitter.com/jblakebooks ⓣ

First published in hardback in 2013
This edition published paperback in 2015

ISBN: 978 1 78418 757 6

British Library Cataloguing-in-Publication Data:

A catalogue record for this book is available from the British Library.

Design by www.envydesign.co.uk

Printed in Great Britain by CPI Group (UK) Ltd

1 3 5 7 9 10 8 6 4 2

The right of A S Dagnell to be identified as the author of this work has been
asserted by him in accordance with the Copyright, Designs and Patents Act 1988.

Papers used by John Blake Publishing are natural, recyclable products
made from wood grown in sustainable forests. The manufacturing processes
conform to the environmental regulations of the country of origin.

Every attempt has been made to contact the relevant copyright-holders,
but some were unobtainable. We would be grateful if the appropriate people
could contact us.

# Acknowledgements

I have drawn on various newspaper articles from the last 20 years as part of my research for this book.

In particular the following newspapers, their supplements, magazines and news sources have been especially helpful: *Daily Mirror, Sunday Mirror, Daily Mail, Mail on Sunday, Daily Telegraph, Sunday Telegraph, Daily Express, Sunday Express, Financial Times, Sunday People, Independent, Independent on Sunday, The Times, The Sunday Times, Guardian, The New York Times, Sun, Scotsman, Observer, Kentish Gazette, Leicester Mercury, The Grocer, Radio Times, Liverpool Echo, Liverpool Post, Wirral News* and the Press Association.

On top of that there have been a number of blogs and websites that have been useful in the writing of this biography. These include: Wikipedia, ArtisanBaker.com,

Love Productions' website, CBS and the BBC's website, and the websites of the various hotels where Paul has worked over the years.

In addition, Paul's appearances on *The Great British Bake Off*, *The American Baking Competition* and *Paul Hollywood's Bread* have of course been a rich source of information and anecdotes.

## THANKS

First of all, Emma Barrow. You've helped me immeasurably with ideas and input for this book and, as you know, I'm hugely grateful. You're one in a million. Thanks for the continuous support and encouragement.

Clive Hebard, thank you once again for being a really supportive editor throughout this whole book. As ever, your experience and knowledge have been invaluable while writing it. Between us I think we probably know everything you could ever need to know about baking and *The Great British Bake Off*.

Everyone at John Blake Publishing, thanks for your continued help and the work you keep putting my way. In particular, thanks to John Blake, Rosie Virgo, Allie Collins, Liz Mallett, Clare Tillyer and Joanna Kennedy.

And my family – Mum, Dad and Nicole. You're always hugely supportive and I really appreciate it.

# Contents

Chapter 1    Britain's Best-Loved Baker    1

Chapter 2 - Liquid Yeast Running Through His Veins    11

Chapter 3 - The Royal Seal of Approval    29

Chapter 4 - Six Years in Cyprus    43

Chapter 5 - Back In Blighty    59

Chapter 6 - In the Dough    75

Chapter 7 - The *Bake Off* Takes Off    93

Chapter 8 - The *Bake Off* Continues    111

Chapter 9 - Greatest Judging Duo in History    127

Chapter 10 - The George Clooney of Baking    143

Chapter 11 - Baking For Blokes    159

Chapter 12 – Paul Goes to Hollywood       175
Chapter 13 – A Heartbreaking Twist        193
Chapter 14 – Testing Times                209
Chapter 15 – Bread, Buns and Baking       225
Chapter 16 – The Future                   247

# CHAPTER 1

# Britain's Best-Loved Baker

It should have been a blissful, triumphant moment in Paul Hollywood's life. He was returning to the UK and his life had changed forever. As he sat on the transatlantic jetliner he must have been thinking about how much he had changed. One moment he was running a successful bakery business. A baker by trade, he had grown up around bread, croissants and pastries. His whole family had baked – both for fun and to make an honest living. And Paul had followed in their footsteps from a young age. But he had taken baking to a whole new level, for in a short space of time he had managed to cross over to become one of Britain's fastest-rising TV stars. BBC bosses had recruited him to be the face of a new series that had become an overnight hit. *The Great British Bake Off* had flown in the ratings and alongside the doyenne of British baking, Mary Berry, Paul had become the face of the series, judging a string of contestants on their various bakes as they vied to become Britain's next big baker. He had gone from being a master baker to Britain's next big telly chef.

And then, as if that wasn't enough, life was about to take a dramatic turn. But not all of it was good. After wrapping up the third series of *The Great British Bake Off* in 2012, rumours suddenly started circulating. First, newspapers were reporting that the hit British series was going stateside. That was nothing out of the ordinary; it was a well-trodden path for successful homegrown TV shows, like *X Factor* and *Strictly Come Dancing*, to be rolled out in the United States. But next the tabloids began linking Paul to the new US series. Would he reprise his role in the US show? Was this the start of a glitzy Hollywood career (for Hollywood)? And if he took the job, would he turn his back on the British version of the show?

The truth was that Paul *would* sign for the CBS series. Amid all the speculation and hearsay, he signed on the dotted line to reprise his role as a judge on the American version of *Bake Off*, aptly named *The American Baking Competition*. Here was a true rags-to-riches tale. For the baker's son from the Wirral, who had started out in the family business, it was monumental for he was now on the verge of becoming a household name in the States with the world at his feet. Naturally, he was brimming with enthusiasm for his new role. 'I think it's going to be fantastic,' he told the *Sun* newspaper. 'They've got things like Mississippi mud pie and pumpkin pie. They're known for their baking so I think it will be a great success.'

The quote underlined all that Hollywood was about. Yes, it was hugely exciting to be launched as a TV star in the US. It would bring huge opportunities for himself and his supportive wife Alexandra and their young son Joshua. But more importantly, it was all about the baking. The fact that the first thing he was to focus on when describing the pros of being involved in the American series is the delight he would feel when exploring the different types of baking recipes that would be available shows just how much he cared.

For him baking had become a way of life. His enthusiasm, dedication and commitment are second to none. These qualities have made him Britain's best-loved baker. It's hard to imagine that anyone cares more about producing a tasty sourdough or baking a fresh batch of scones than Paul Hollywood   other than his *Bake Off* co-presenter, Mary Berry, of course, but his professional baking background is what sets him apart. It was his passion for his craft, alongside his popular appeal, that had propelled him to stardom and secured him what was speculated to be a lucrative contract in the US.

Now, as the summer of 2013 was fast approaching, he filmed his first series of *The American Baking Competition*. All was set for the launch of the show on 29 May. With his commitments complete, Paul made the trip back to the UK. And as he sat on the airplane bound for London, you might imagine that he was feeling more content than ever. With stateside success in the offing, surely this was a time for celebration?

Not quite. For Paul was heading back to face one of the toughest times of his life. His 15-year marriage to his wife

Alexandra had hit the rocks, and within days the British newspapers would break the story of their separation. This would undoubtedly be a testing time and cast a dark shadow over what should have been an incredible highlight in his career.

But this wasn't a straightforward separation, for the tabloids quickly linked the break-up to Paul's apparent close friendship with his new co-judge on *The American Baking Competition* – the young, pretty, glamorous Mexican-born Marcela Valladolid, 13 years his junior. The press speculated as to whether he and Marcela were indeed an item and even suggested they were planning to move in together. A media storm would erupt, with his whole reputation at stake. And there was nothing he could do to stop it – not even via his prolific use of the social networking site Twitter, where he would regularly connect with his fans and on which he kept an uncannily low profile as the news broke. It was testament to the fickle nature of celebrity; one minute you are everyone's hero, the next it could all turn to rubble.

He himself had become only too aware of how quickly his life was changing. In one interview with the *Sunday Mirror*, he reflected on how much his stardom had risen in just 12 months of being on *The Great British Bake Off*. 'It is quite cultish, isn't it?' he said, almost naively, not realising the full extent to which the show had grown – almost tripling its viewing figures over the course of three series. 'It's all about timing,' he went on to say, 'when you become a product of a big programme, you get busier and it's hard trying to fit everything in. I am just really enjoying myself.'

But as the tabloids continued to lay into him and to speculate on his love life for weeks on end, the timing couldn't have been worse. What should have been a huge moment in his career was truly overshadowed by the tabloid machine.

The truth was that Paul's apparent sex appeal was what seemed to be setting him apart as a star. At the very least, it was winning him scores of admirers. In the previous year leading up to the launch of *The American Baking Competition*, female feature writers constantly celebrated his charisma and charm, as well as his undoubted good looks, within the pages of the British press. One writer in the *Daily Telegraph* even went so far as to describe his work as 'patisserie porn':

> Close your eyes, ladies. Feel the lightest dusting of icing sugar on your lips, the caress of cream on your tongue, breathe in the heady scent of raspberries and vanilla and – ooh, is that Paco Rabanne? And possibly essence of WD40? Yes, this is real baking by a real man, with the impassive flinty gaze of a Liverpool bouncer and the sensuous hands of Christian Grey. May I present to you Paul Hollywood, Britain's most unlikely pin-up. Twitter is a-flutter, the racy opinions on Mumsnet would make a navvie blush and last weekend, when the *Daily Telegraph* included his 'Fifty Shades of Granary' supplement, there were practically riots in newsagents the length of the land.

It seemed that a big part of Paul's appeal was that he wasn't just a good-looking man but one who could bake too! As one writer explained: 'Hollywood's twinkly appeal, coupled with the fact that Britons gobble 3.25 billion loaves a year, is a tempting concoction.'

Nevertheless, despite his rapid rise to fame, Paul seemed to be taking everything in his stride, even if fame and all its trappings were not necessarily something he always felt comfortable with. 'I'll admit I am a bit of a show-off but I'm actually shy,' he told the *Daily Express*. 'The guy on TV is the guy I hide behind. I do get stage fright. I'm shaking till I walk out and then this twin takes over. Obviously you're there to teach but you can't just stand there spouting instructions. You've got to entertain people and it's hard work. I'm exhausted at the end.'

His newfound fame meant that he needed security at large events. And he was suddenly being mobbed by hundreds of autograph hunters. 'I don't want it, but it's necessary,' he insisted. 'I'm always happy to sign autographs or [to] have my photo taken but if you stop for one person, before you know it they're 10 to 15 deep around you and I'm supposed to be somewhere else but I can't move. I'll shout out, "I will sign if you come back after" as I'm being bundled away.'

The truth was that after three series of steadily building success, *The Great British Bake Off* had become a national phenomenon, inspiring home bakers the length and breadth of the country to dust off their aprons and start kneading their first batch of dough while encouraging those already partial to a bit of home baking to up their game and try some of the more ambitious recipes from the series. It seemed Paul was in great demand, though even he couldn't quite get his head around how quickly it had all happened. To begin with, neither could the critics, but they quickly came on board. 'On paper *Great British Bake Off* sounds like a daft idea, at best fit for nothing more than the most brain-dead slot in the daytime TV schedules,' wrote Anna Pukas in the *Daily Express*. 'Yet its success has been nothing short of astounding. The first series in 2010 started with 2.4 million viewers and ended with 3.8 million, while for the second last year ratings shot up from 3.6 to 5.1 million. This series is averaging 5 million viewers.' Or, as Paul put it more plainly, 'It's gone completely mental.'

Soon he would be such hot property that features would be written about his hair, with one writer from the *Weekend Argus* demanding she be allowed to touch it:

Let us be clear from the outset, I don't insist upon stroking the hair of everyone I meet. If I did, I would be writing this on pieces of tracing paper that I had secreted under the mattress of the bunk in my cell. But when you meet Paul Hollywood, you can't help yourself. It's like giving in to the urge to tweak the cheek of an alabaster cherub in a museum, or stroke the delicate folds of the ballet skirt on a Degas ballerina.

He had the female viewing public, as well as the critics, eating out of the palm of his hand. The close bond that he had formed with his co-presenter, baking guru Mary Berry, on the series had cemented his reputation as a 'nice guy'. It seemed Mary's welfare was of paramount importance to him, and in the course of one interview, journalist Sarah Chalmers from the *Daily Mail* noticed how Paul, usually so cool, calm and collected, only became on edge when she mentioned the possibility of Mary leaving the *Bake Off*. 'After a momentary pause,' she wrote, 'he replies, "She'll go on forever."'

And it was their interpersonal chemistry that truly set them apart as one of the best judging duos on British reality TV: Paul was bad cop to Mary's good cop. It was a routine that worked wonders on screen. While Mary was always more sympathetic, even if the bakes she was judging had been an unmitigated disaster, Paul was far blunter, in the process earning himself a reputation as the 'Simon Cowell of the baking world'. But as far as he was concerned, he was just delivering an honest opinion. 'It's not personal, it's just about what they do,' he told the *Scottish Daily Record*. 'Some programmes have a pop at the person themselves but I give an honest opinion and maybe they've never had an honest opinion before. That's part of it and, if they get upset, it's a good thing. If they didn't get upset I'd be more worried. If they did nothing, they're never going to get better.'

He was also of the view that the differences between himself and Mary only made their on-screen relationship stronger. 'Mary came from a home cooking background and I came from a professional baking background,' he explained. 'I won't make one cake, I'll make 50. So I'll look at it from a business point of view.' Indeed he would often say how much he has learned from Mary, thanks to their differing approaches.

Paul's greatest asset, though, is his directness. When it comes to judging, he calls a spade a spade. Little wonder he would later reveal that friends and family often become nervous around him when presenting him with cakes. 'Friends ask me to judge their bakes now, and I sometimes get embarrassed,' he told the *Sun*. 'I was at a party recently and the hostess asked me to judge a cake she'd made. I tried to put her off but she insisted – so I admitted the cake was a bit dry round the edges and had sunk in the middle. She didn't speak to me for weeks.'

On another occasion he attended a cake sale at his 11-year-old son Joshua's school. And you can imagine the panic that descended on the other parents. 'My son's school had a cake sale in the playground recently and you could see everyone panicking when I arrived,' he told the *Daily Mail*. 'They all watched to see what I'd go for. I bought a particularly good lemon drizzle cake, and I'm sure the mother who made it is still living off the story!'

Like father, like son, Joshua is also proving to be a keen baker. Paul recounted to the *Sunday Express*: 'Our son, Josh – who's 11 this year – is the same. He's also got a fine palate and will tell you if you haven't put enough Parmesan in a risotto. He's also a great little baker and I've made cupcakes and pizzas with him. He wanted to compete in *Junior Bake Off*. There were loads of tears when I said, "I'm your dad. It's not going to happen, son..."'

Without doubt, Paul's reputation as a master baker was beginning to precede him. When it came to breads, buns and baking per se, he was a genius. No one could fault what he could produce with a bit of dough and an oven. But now it seemed that his reputation was being called into question. As his marriage ran into difficulties suddenly questions were being asked in a whole string of newspaper stories. So, was he as nice a guy as everyone first thought? What would happen to his career? And would his personal life affect the success of the British and US *Bake Off* shows? Or would the series continue to go from strength to strength?

And most important of all, would Paul remain Britain's best-loved baker?

Only time would tell.

# CHAPTER 2

# Liquid Yeast Running Through His Veins

As the newest and most up-and-coming star of the quintessentially middle class world of home baking, you might imagine that Paul Hollywood comes from a similar background himself. In fact, nothing could be further from the truth. While his star turns on *The Great British Bake Off* sent him on a stellar trajectory that would see him conquer TV land in the UK, and hopefully on the other side of the Atlantic where an American version of the show was to be launched, making him a household name in the well-appointed living rooms of millions, it's fair to say he comes from humble, working-class roots. They are roots that Paul, no matter how successful he becomes, has never forgotten and never will.

Born in 1966, he grew up Wallasey, on Merseyside, and was the eldest of three brothers born to his parents, John and

Gill. And it seems that his fate was sealed from the get-go. John himself was a baker by trade, and Paul and his brothers were brought up in a flat above one of the bakeries that he owned. From an early age, Paul was introduced to the joys of freshly baked bread, cakes of all different shapes and sizes, pastries and biscuits. John was an incredibly hard worker. After setting up the bakery over which he and his family lived, he would gradually expand the business to open up a string of other shops in and around the Liverpool area, and later across other regions of Britain. Indeed his father's guiding principles of good baking and a solid work ethic proved a steady influence throughout Paul's formative years and his early adult life.

John would work around the clock building up the first bakery business, which served hundreds of people in the local community – everything from traditional daily staples such as loaves of bread and rolls to more elaborate cakes and biscuits. One can only assume he was something of a legend in the area as he soon became part of the locals' daily routines as they popped by on their way to work or during their lunch hour. 'Dad was always in bed in the afternoons because of getting up in the early hours to bake,' Paul recalled in an interview with the *Daily Mail*.

Yet as a young boy, the early mornings were something that perhaps dissuaded him from following in father's footsteps – in the beginning at least. 'It's one of the reasons I didn't want to be a baker initially,' he explained in the same interview. 'I was a bed person. I think most teenagers are. But eventually you realise that getting up at dawn on a summer morning is the best time. The roads are quiet, you can think and you work while everyone else is sleeping.'

But it wasn't just John who had a penchant for baked goods. Although Paul's mum Gill would work from home as a graphic artist by day, she also threw herself into baking whenever she could during her spare time. Some of Paul's earliest memories are of Gill cooking up a sweet treat for him and his brothers, which they would almost certainly devour when they returned home from school. Paul has revealed that one of his most vivid memories is of when he was just five years old and his mum got him involved in making a big batch of ginger biscuits.

He told the *Daily Telegraph*: 'Ginger biscuits, golden-brown and cookie-like, were the first things I ever made with my mother. She hated cooking but loved baking and was great with pastry. She used a basic recipe: just golden syrup, powdered ginger, butter and self-raising flour. I remember making little balls with the dough and flattening them down with my grubby little hands. We used a fork to make a pattern on the top. I don't remember my two brothers being there, though they must have been. Maybe I've blocked them out of my mind, as you do with younger brothers! The baking time, about 15 minutes on gas mark four, was torturous for me – the smell! Because of all the butter in them they came out with a bend rather than a snap and were truly delicious.'

He went on to recall an early memory of bread: 'One Saturday afternoon – I know it was a Saturday because *Dr Who* was on – Dad made white rolls. I remember shaping them with him. He left them on a tray covered with a towel in front of the fire and I was fascinated, peeking under the towel to watch the pockets of air grow. When he baked them the smell filled the house. It's the smell of baking that I remember most from my childhood.'

Gill, he would later recall, would also whip up a delicious apple pie. 'My mum is a great baker,' he told the *Liverpool Echo*. 'She makes the best apple pie I've ever tasted. She has a real skill with sweet things. My dad gave me my love of savoury – his bread is fantastic. I was very lucky – I've been baking for as long as I can remember. I think it must be in the blood.'

It certainly appeared to be the case. While baking was a huge part of both his parents' lives, it was something that seemed to run in the Hollywood family too. Paul fondly recalls how his nan would also work wonders in the kitchen, regularly producing a classic Victoria sponge. Funnily enough, it was the exact same cake that would become his *Great British Bake Off* co-judge Mary Berry's signature dish in years to come. 'My nan was a great cook too,' he told the *Liverpool Echo*. 'Her Victoria sponge was amazing.'

But the Hollywood family's historic relationship with baking stretched back still further – and in an even more prestigious manner. Paul's maternal grandfather was the head baker at the prestigious Adelphi Hotel. Based in Ranelagh Place, in the heart of Liverpool city centre, the place is steeped in a rich history, rivalled by few other hotels in the area. Today the hotel has been granted a Grade II listing by English Heritage to mark its status as a fine example of Edwardian architecture and interior design. It is now owned by the Britannia Hotels group, who have expanded it to include 402 en-suite bedrooms, as well as conference and dining facilities and a gymnasium. More recently, the hotel rose to prominence in 1997 when it was the subject of a fly-on-the-wall documentary by the BBC, which followed the day-to-day running of the establishment. Called *Hotel*, it came out at a time when similar documentaries were proving popular with viewers. *Airport*, which followed the busy goings-on at London Heathrow, first became a prime time hit the previous year, in the process making a star of Aeroflot supervisor Jeremy Spake, who went on to front his own documentaries.

*Hotel* was very much along the same lines, but instead gave viewers a rare glimpse of what it was like for the staff at the Adelphi. The first series aired on 3 November 1997 on BBC1 and proved a huge ratings hit, taking home 11 million viewers. The stand-out star was hotel manager Eileen Downey, who became popular with viewers thanks to her feisty, no-nonsense personality. Meanwhile, somewhat bizarrely, the phrase 'Just cook, will yer' became a cult phenomenon off the back of the series, after a scene was aired which included an argument between deputy manager Brian Burchill and head chef David Smith. Indeed, the catchphrase became so well known that it was printed on T-shirts and even made its way into the music charts after a track was built around it by Alternative Radio.

But it was a different story when Paul's grandfather worked there. Once construction was complete in 1826, the establishment was opened to great fanfare by the renowned hotelier James Radley. While the building itself went through several incarnations, it was grand enough when it first opened to be regarded as 'the most luxurious hotel outside of London', according to historian Richard Pollard. Public rooms contained columns, marble panelling and coffered arches, while French doors opened into restaurants along the sides. It was, at the time, the epitome of decadence. The pressure on Paul's grandfather to be at the top of his game as the hotel's baker-in-chief would have been immense – and his skill and expertise were doubtless qualities that would filter down through subsequent generations.

Paul's grandfather would have contributed enormously to the hotel's success. Wealthy people would flock to the hotel, not least because Liverpool was a huge hub for those arriving and departing on ocean liners during the early twentieth century. Almost immediately, the Adelphi seemed to become the in place for these visitors to stay before heading out of the UK to far-flung destinations such as the US, Africa and closer to home in Europe. Notable guests include former US President Franklin D. Roosevelt and ex-British Prime Minister Winston Churchill, as well as stars from the world of show business, including singer Frank Sinatra, comedy duo Laurel & Hardy and actress Judy Garland, all of whom would stay at the hotel while performing at the city's world-famous Empire Theatre. Certainly, Paul's grandfather's baking would have had to survive a discerning taste test or two to get past such celebrated guests! Little did he realise, however, that in the years to come, one member of his family would also achieve celebrity status himself.

In addition to his parents and grandfather, Paul's uncles became bakers, while the younger of his two brothers, Lee, also threw himself into bakery, running a successful wholesale baking business once he got older, in Moreton, also on Merseyside.

As writer Anna Pukas put it in the *Daily Express*, 'Paul probably has liquid yeast running through his veins.' And so, as he grew older, it seemed almost inevitable that Paul would inherit the family's baking skills. Aside from helping his mum make biscuits in the kitchen, his first proper introduction to the art of baking started early when he accompanied his father to work during the school holidays. Like many fathers, John would have been trying to give his son a focus during those long weeks away from school. But these trips to work with his dad quickly piqued his interest, which soon turned into something of a hobby. Paul too got the baking bug. While his classmates played football or messed around in the park, Paul would observe John and his team of fellow bakers in rapt awe, savouring every minute as he took the opportunity to learn from his father.

'Every time I went missing I'd be found in the kitchen watching someone at work, my head barely as high as the counter,' he later told the *Daily Mail*.

It wasn't long before Paul started to bake in his spare time too, trying his hand at all sorts of recipes in the professional bakery downstairs from the family flat. While Gill and John would doubtless have been proud of their fast-learning son, there may well have been some regrets too. 'I'd like to say sorry to my mum, Gill, for all the washing I used to give her from the bakery,' Paul told the *Sunday Express*. 'It would be caked with dough and she could never get it clean enough. I used to give her a lot of grief about it.'

But if his parents thought Paul's interest in baking was just a passing phase, they would soon be proved wrong. What started as a means to occupy himself during the school holidays and weekends fast became a way of making money for the enterprising boy. As he hit his teenage years, Paul decided he wanted to take up baking as a part-time job. 'I started making trays and trays of cakes with my dad when he worked at Blake's Cakes,' he told the *Liverpool Echo*. Soon he developed a niche. 'By the time I was a teenager I had a Saturday job jamming doughnuts with a big machine, which was really satisfying,' he told the *Daily Mail*. But things didn't always go to plan. At the age of 13, Paul somehow managed to mix up the ingredients while preparing a batch of dough-nuts. And it ended with him coating 1,000 doughnuts with salt instead of sugar! Suffice to say, John was not amused. 'He docked my wages for a month after that,' laughed Paul in an interview with the *Liverpool Echo*. But like most novices, he learnt the error of his ways. 'I never made that mistake again,' he added.

Over time, he went from strength to strength, graduating from doughnuts to become an accomplished baker. 'I'd do sponges, trays of flies' graveyards – that's what we called the currant cakes,' he told the *Liverpool Echo*. 'Then I went on to croissants, and I really started to get into it.' It seemed there was no stopping the young Hollywood as he wholeheartedly embraced his family's love of baking. Surely his career was now set in stone? Well no, not quite. Paul, it seemed, had other ideas...

It's important to remember that Paul grew up in a heavily industrialised part of the country, where it wasn't the norm to become a baker but to take up a very different type of manual labour: working in Wallasey's busy dockyards. Nestled in Merseyside, Wallasey town is famous for its links with shipping, heavy industry and docks. It's not, therefore, somewhere you'd imagine a love for baking fine breads and sweet treats would typically be born. Looking back through Wallasey's rich industrial history, it's easy to imagine Paul might have followed a path into a blue-collar manual job, carrying out heavy labour in the town's shipping docks rather than kneading dough in chef's whites.

Sitting at the mouth of the River Mersey on the north-eastern corner of the Wirral Peninsula, Wallasey became the focus of the Mersey's expansion of trade during the late nineteenth century, with new docks being constructed between 1842 and 1847 in the Wallasey Pool in response to increased trade on the Mersey. By 1877, the dock system between Wallasey and nearby Birkenhead was complete. In the years that followed, the region became one of Britain's focal points when it came to engineering industries, in particular shipbuilding, sugar refinery and cement and fertiliser manufacturing. Not surprisingly, the docks provided a huge proportion of jobs, and many of Paul's predecessors would have easily found work, thanks to these heavy industries that became the lifeblood of the community.

But while many of his peers would almost certainly have been taking up apprenticeships in more manual-based, labouring jobs, it wasn't local industry that would lure Paul away from bakery. It seemed he was determined to rebel against going into the family profession – for a short while at least. After progressing through school, he decided that he wanted to be an artist. As careers go, nothing could be further from what might have been expected of him growing up in such a tough area, but it seemed he was determined to rebel and to forge a very different path. Like a lot of teenagers, he seemed to have no desire to conform, and he made the bold decision to go against the grain.

By now it was the early 80s and hippy-chic was all the rage. Paul, whose friends called him 'PJ' for short (his middle name was John after his dad), embraced the new trend and the life of an artist. He grew his hair long, halfway down his back. Having enrolled in a foundation course in sculpture at the Wallasey College of Art, he threw himself into it, but very soon the prospect of being a penniless bohemian with few job prospects and no regular income began to wear thin. Whether he would admit it or not, baking was clearly something that he could make a very decent living out of – even if he didn't realise, aged 18, quite how good an income he would eventually generate.

For the time being, however, his dad made him an offer that he couldn't refuse. 'He said if I jacked it in and worked for him instead he'd give me £500, but only as long as I cut my hair,' Paul told the *Daily Mail* in a later interview. 'That was a lot of cash in the mid-80s.' In his typically direct manner –

which Paul seemed to adopt himself years later as the straight-talking judge on *The Great British Bake Off* – he recalled how John had said to him: 'Look, son, I'll give you £500 if you quit college, cut your hair and join the family bakery.' Money talked, and just as fast as he had taken up his course in sculpture, it was given the chop – along with his hair – in favour of working full-time in the family business.

It was a decision he would not regret; indeed he has admitted that he's never looked back since working for his father. To begin with, Paul worked in the family bakeries, which had now opened up across Merseyside in Bootle, Anfield and Walton. Like any other youngster starting out in his career, he had to work long hours as he mastered the intricacies of his trade. The home baking that he would have enjoyed with his mum, as well as the weekend work with Dad, would have provided a great foundation, but he now had to hone his craft, like any other apprentice. In particular, he needed to get used to the customers' specific requests, such as the way they liked their bread prepared. One particular trait that Paul picked up on was that his fellow Merseysiders seemed to have a penchant for a slightly over-cooked loaf.

'Liverpool is different,' he once told the *Daily Mail*. 'They like a bit of burnt here. When I worked in Dad's bakery, an old dear would always come in and say: "Listen love, can you stick it in the back of the oven and burn it for ten minutes." She's right – I like it crusty and dark myself.'

Paul's passion for baking clearly shone through, and before long his father decided it was time for his responsibilities to be extended. Coincidentally John had opened a new bakery away from Merseyside, in Lincoln near the east coast of England. It seemed the perfect opportunity to give his son the chance to step up to the plate and start managing one of the bakeries by himself. And so John dispatched Paul to Lincoln, where he was placed in charge of the shop, running it solo. No doubt he would have employed exactly the same work ethic as witnessed in his father all those years ago.

Of course he was only too aware that he would have to make sacrifices along the way, given the baking industry was such a labour-intensive job. While his friends would be out all hours, Paul has admitted that he had to force himself to take early nights and be up well before dawn to get fresh loaves in the oven, ready for the morning rush. 'My mates would go clubbing and stop by the bakery in the early hours for something to eat,' he recalled in an interview with the *Daily Mail*. Regardless, he now knew that baking was his passion. 'It upset me a bit to miss out on partying, but baking was what I wanted to do,' he added.

'I lost all my youth to my trade,' he later revealed in an interview with the Northern Irish newspaper, the *Sunday Life*. 'I chose to have a career. Most of the lads I worked with are still living in the Wirral in Liverpool [...] That was my decision and I lost my youth to it. I used to go to bed at six o'clock in the evening and all my mates were going out but that was my choice. I wanted to be the best – that was my ambition. Whatever I do, I want to be the best. I'm very competitive.'

But his drive never dented the close bond with the friends he grew up with in Wallasey, and in recent newspaper interviews, he still talks about the fact that some of his closest buddies to this day are the ones he met while growing up on the Wirral. 'My best friend is my mate Chris Davies from Wallasey, where I grew up,' he told one reporter from the *Sunday Express*. 'We still see each other when I go up to the Wirral to visit family.' Like a lot of lads he was becoming increasingly aware of the opposite sex too – even if the romances, when he was young at least, were fleeting. 'My first kiss was when I was 14,' he told the *Sunday Express*. 'I can't remember her name but it was outside this girl's house and not very memorable. That romance didn't last long.'

And so from humble beginnings Paul started to forge a career for himself in the family baking business. And he certainly has a lot to thank baking for. After all, if he hadn't abandoned a sculpture course at Wallasey School of Art to go and work in his dad's bakery on the other side of the country, he would never have ended up on the path that led to *The Great British Bake Off*. One of Paul's most admirable qualities is that today he remains as passionate about Liverpool as when he was growing up and still finding his feet. Over the years, Merseyside has experienced some tough times; struggling through the doom and gloom of the recession and feeling the pinch of the British economy's woes, which have seen countless small businesses scaled back or completely shut down. To this day, he talks passionately about wanting to keep baking alive and kicking in Merseyside, and he constantly tries to inspire youngsters in the area to follow in his footsteps. He believes that if he can encourage a new generation of young bakers in the region, the industry stands a good chance of survival. 'Food is a great basis for rejuvenating any area,' he told one reporter from the *Liverpool Echo*. 'If people start to understand food better and develop the skills to get into the trade, then they can follow in the footsteps of someone like [Kirkby-born chef] Aiden Byrne, who has done phenomenally well.'

In recent years Liverpool has been through something of a renaissance. It was named one of the European Capitals of Culture 2008 (alongside Norway's Stavanger), which saw funds poured into the city to finance redevelopment, once more encouraging prosperity. Being the homebody that he is, Paul remains loyal to the Wirral and constantly champions the area that he believes may have been neglected in favour of its more cosmopolitan neighbours. 'I think Wirral has been kicked in the teeth because all the money is being spent in Liverpool,' he said in one interview with the *Liverpool Echo*. 'It is sad when you drive around – it needs an injection of something. I went to Liscard recently and it was just shops saying "bargain" and "saver" and "cheque clearance". In New Brighton they are building a casino! Why does it need that? I remember when it had a pool and an indoor fairground and a tower. We need someone who understands the area to take it on because everyone around here works hard and deserves better.'

Doubtless he is keen to champion the Wirral because of the fantastic start in life that it gave him. But even while the area may have been down on its luck in recent years, Paul remains confident that it can produce even more excellent bakers in the years to come. For him, baking and cooking more generally is not an elite industry requiring an expensive education or contacts with those in the know to get one's foot in the door. Even a boy from Wallasey who was brought up above a bakery can reach the top of his game with enough hard work. He maintains success in the baking industry is not something that depends on having the best qualifications from the premier catering colleges in the country. So long as you have the determination to succeed, peppered with a small amount of creativity, an ability to learn and sufficient competence, you can go all the way. Frequently in interviews, he comes across as being proud of his humble beginnings: 'I came from a normal background,' he once said. 'But if you have the flair and the passion, you can do whatever you want with food. If lads and girls want to be a chef, there are plenty of places looking for talent. To get on a show like *The Great British Bake Off*, you have to be good. Personally I want to see people on there representing our area with a strong accent, driving everyone mad.'

The fact that he makes regular trips to Merseyside to support the local food and drink industry is testament to his loyalty to the area. One year, for example, Paul volunteered his services to present the coveted Liverpool Food & Drink Awards. It fell to him to announce the 11 winners in categories such as Liverpool's Favourite Producer, Favourite Independent Cafe/Coffee Shop, Favourite Restaurant and Favourite Bar or Pub. Supporters of more than 70 bars, restaurants and producers from around the city were set to descend on the arts venue The Camp & Furnace following weeks of public voting. More than 3,000 votes were cast in just under eight weeks, the culmination of the Liverpool Food & Drink Festival. Paul was once again keen to champion local talent. 'The city seems to have evolved into an extraordinary culinary hotspot over recent years,' he noted at the event. 'The talent within the industry is outstanding and it will be interesting to see who was voted the public's favourite.'

It wasn't the only time that he used his culinary expertise to return to his Merseyside roots in recent years. Off the back of his success in *The Great British Bake Off*, he staged a local version of the search to discover outstanding kitchen creations in September 2012. The aptly named The Great Merseyside Bake Off was also part of the same food and drink festival and called on amateurs across the region to get baking and submit photos of their homemade cakes to a judging panel. The best 12 were then invited to take part in a live bake off, which took place in the historic Sefton Park. Naturally it fell to Paul to oversee the panel. After all, it seemed only fitting that he should return to his place of birth to share the skill that has made him a celebrity – judging baked goods. 'There's so much talent in the region, I've been keen to run a battle of the bakers here for a while,' he told the *Wirral News*. 'I think the Liverpool Food & Drink Festival will provide a perfect setting for the bake off, which will be great fun.'

And what was the winner's prize in The Great Merseyside Bake Off? Well, it wasn't quite on a par with winning *The Great British Bake Off*, but it was still two tickets to the festival, where the winner lifted a trophy in front of Merseyside's top talent from the world of food and drink. On top of that, the winning recipe featured as 'Cake of the

Month' in the café of large department store John Lewis in the swanky Liverpool ONE shopping centre right in the heart of the city. All those who took part in the competition will no doubt be eyeing up the chance to apply for Paul's other *Bake Off* too – if they get that far!

Even if he's not taking part in a festival or judging a local competition, Paul is keen to return to Merseyside as often as he can. After all, it's the place where he first discovered his love of baking. And so it's unquestionable that he has never, and will never, forget where he comes from, despite national success on TV and with his books, which have made him famous on both sides of the Atlantic. But before all that could happen, Paul was to break into baking on a different scale – at some of the country's finest hotels.

# CHAPTER 3

# The Royal Seal
# of Approval

Working for his father, first across the Wirral and later managing other bakeries on England's east coast, was the best apprenticeship Paul could ask for. He had mastered the basics of his trade and what had begun as a hobby was now starting to resemble a career. After a few years of working for his dad, he was ready for a new challenge. 'I was passionate and very competitive,' he told the *Daily Mail*. 'I wanted to become the best. Mix passion with a competitive streak and ambition and you've got a recipe to do whatever you want. Anyone who's successful will have one or all three of those traits.'

With drive and commitment such as this, it was no wonder he would quickly rise through the ranks. And an opportunity soon presented itself that would catapult him from working in local bakeries to far grander locations altogether. A job was advertised at the Chester Grosvenor – and he seized the opportunity with both hands. The hotel was well known in the northwest of England for being one of the very best. With an unrivalled reputation for excellence, it was a popular destination for anyone who was anyone when visiting Chester. And now they were looking for a baker to join their kitchen. For Paul it was his dream job and a logical next step up the career ladder. He knew only too well the rich history of the hotel, which stretched back to the nineteenth century. The plot of land where this formidable establishment now stands was purchased by Robert Grosvenor who, at the time, was the Earl Grosvenor but would later become the 1st Marquess of Westminster. Interestingly, the building was actually the headquarters of the then powerful Independent party, who at the time were apparently opposed to the Grosvenor family. Whether it was an act of revenge or otherwise to buy the building, Robert Grosvenor decided it would be better used as a hotel and quickly set about his project. The building was demolished and a new one built in its place before being named the Grosvenor Hotel. According to Simon Ward's *Chester: A History*, it became known as the 'premier place to stay' in the town.

The hotel itself is something of an architectural masterpiece. In January 1972 it was registered as a Grade II listed building – and it's easy to see how this came about. Originally designed by Thomas Mainwaring Penson, a local surveyor and architect, it was to be his last major project before his death in 1864. Over the years Penson has been credited with the renewed fashion for half-timbered or black-and-white buildings in Chester, which he reintroduced during the course of his career. Sadly he passed away before the Grosvenor Hotel project could be completed, but the task of bringing his vision to life was left to his son's firm, R. K. Penson & Ritchie. The building itself has held on to some of the original features. Today it still displays Penson's passion for timber, half in black and half in white, in keeping with the Tudor revival to be seen throughout Chester.

Once the freshening up and rebuild was complete, the hotel was then passed on to the estate of the Duke of Westminster in 1874. By then it was Richard's son, Hugh Grosvenor, who was now the 1st Duke of Westminster.

The hotel opened in the historic location of Eastgate in the very heart of Chester. It sits in pride of place next to the Eastgate Clock and close to Grosvenor Park, Chester Cathedral and the city's ancient walls. With the doors now open and guests flowing through, the family set about cementing its reputation as one of the finest in the northwest. Today, the hotel has a five-star rating and is consistently voted the people's favourite in the area. So when Paul came to work for the Chester Grosvenor, he would have had to rise to the challenge. No longer was it just about baking as many products as possible as previously in his father's bakeries; now a whole new level of service was expected of him to meet the demands of an elite clientele. According to tourism websites, the hotel boasts 68 guest bedrooms, as well as 12 sumptuous suites. As well as indulging in Paul's delicious patisserie, guests were free to spend time in a fitness centre, spa, lounge and bar; boardrooms were available for corporate events and parties.

But Paul's work was reserved for the highly acclaimed restaurants. The hotel boasts a Parisian-style family restaurant – La Brasserie – for which he would doubtless have been expected to create croissants, pains au chocolat and gâteaux as good as any to be found across the French capital. Alongside this relaxed eatery, the hotel also opened another restaurant for more formal long lunches and evening meals: Simon Radley at the Chester Grosvenor. Unsurprisingly, it was named after the hotel's head chef, who took up the reins after joining in 1986. Originally called The Arkle, the name was changed in 2008 to reflect the personal touch that Radley brought to it. In 2011, this success was capped off when the hotel was awarded a Michelin star for the twenty-first year in a row, making it one of only five restaurants across the whole of the UK to hold the coveted star for that many years. Reports in the press state that it's the only restaurant located in the north of England to have managed to achieve such a feat. And with its reputation sky high, little wonder that the establishment has attracted some impressive guests over the years, including Princess Diana and the Prince of Wales, while HM The Queen also visited the hotel when it hosted the wedding celebrations for one of the Grosvenor daughters.

And so, for a working-class boy from the Wirral, bagging a position at the Chester Grosvenor as a junior baker was no mean feat. While Paul would almost certainly have been nervous at the prospect of stepping away from the familiarity of the family business to work for such an esteemed establishment, he knew in his heart that it was an opportunity too good to turn down. He gave up working for his dad and took the plunge, working his way up from the bottom rung of the ladder. So while he started on simple French bakes, his eye for detail and perfectionist tendencies soon got him noticed. He was then tasked with more important responsibilities such as cakes and doing the afternoon teas.

It was while working at the Chester Grosvenor that he got his first taste of what it would be like to be on television. Despite being just 19 years old, the local TV news show, *Granada Reports*, wanted to do a piece on baking bread and they thought Paul might be perfect for the segment. Whether they chose him as a result of his growing reputation in Chester, or it was purely happy accident that he was selected, we will never know. Nevertheless he was delighted to be chosen. The experience also gave him an insight into the harsh realities of TV. 'They interviewed me for about six hours, and I remember thinking as I walked out of the hotel to go home, "I've made it,"' he told the *Radio Times* years later in an interview to publicise *The Great British Bake Off*. Unfortunately, this wasn't to be the case, for the piece finally broadcast turned out to be about 30 seconds long. TV fame may have eluded him on this occasion, but little did he realise that some 20 years later he would be conducting interviews to promote a show that he, and all those involved, would be truly proud of.

Still in his late teens, he was nonetheless succeeding. Little wonder the Chester Grosvenor still has a special place in his heart all these years on. Whenever he is back in the northwest,

Paul finds time to visit the hotel. 'I loved it there,' he has said. 'I still go back there when I'm in town and have their afternoon tea. They're good at doing the little touches so it feels like a real treat.'

But after some time at the Chester Grosvenor, Paul was ready to move on and eager for a new challenge. Next, he took up a job at Cliveden House in Berkshire. Cliveden was, and still is, considered one of the finest houses ever to be built in Britain. Originally designed by Sir Charles Barry in 1851 to replace a house destroyed by a fire, the three-storey mansion has a 400ft by 20ft brick terrace, an original feature dating back to the mid-seventeenth century. The exterior was given a major overhaul between 1984 and 1986, with the work carried out by the National Trust. Modifications include a new lead roof. This took place once the property was acquired by Blakeney Hotels (later Cliveden Hotel Limited) in 1984.

The takeover was driven by the company chairman John Lewis and managing director John Tham, who is married to the actress Jenny Agutter. They oversaw the restoration and refurbishment of the interior, filling the rooms with Edwardian antiques. Today the house is run in a similar style to when Nancy Astor was chatelaine. In 1990 an indoor swimming pool and spa treatment rooms were added within the confines of a pretty walled garden; a new 100-year lease was signed too. More bedrooms were converted, bringing the total to 37; two new dining rooms were also completed. It is considered one of the finest hotels in Britain and frequently listed as one of the most sought-after places to stay.

Among other claims to fame was the fact that it offered the

'world's most expensive sandwich' – at an eye-watering £100 in 2007, the Von Essen Platinum Club Sandwich was confirmed by Guinness World Records to be the costliest sandwich commercially available. The holding company for the Cliveden was later taken over by Von Essen Hotels, which later collapsed in 2011. Nonetheless, Cliveden was widely considered to be the 'Jewel in the Crown' and subsequently snapped up in February 2012 by Richard and Ian Livingston, owners of the well-respected London & Regional Properties. Together they sought to ensure the future of the hotel, placing it under the management of Andrew Stembridge from Chewton Glen, a sister hotel within the same group.

Nowadays the hotel's motto is 'Nothing ordinary ever happened here, nor could it', which fittingly describes how this grand and spectacular establishment has come to be viewed. It was in 1961 in an outdoor swimming pool at Cliveden where former Secretary of State for War John Profumo met Christine Keeler, the reputed mistress of an alleged Soviet spy, leading to one of the biggest scandals in British history. Today the hotel's sumptuous gardens make it ideal for weddings, for which parts are regularly hired out. Meanwhile, the house itself is in perfect condition, following a programme of renovation and redecoration. The property featured in the 2005 film *Mrs Henderson Presents* starring the Oscar-winning actress Dame Judi Dench. Cliveden has been used as a backdrop for other works of film and television including the second Beatles film, *Help!* (released in 1965), where it stood in for Buckingham Palace. The main gates appear in the 1978 movie *Death on the Nile*, while

*Thunderbirds* (2004) sees Cliveden used as the location for Lady Penelope's house, Creighton-Ward Mansion. Literary works also refer to the house, including Daniel Defoe's *A Tour Through England and Wales*, first published in 1726, in which he describes the first house.

So it's fair to say that when Paul says he 'baked at some of the best hotels in the world', as he did in one interview with the *Daily Mail*, it is certainly the case. This particular job had come about thanks to a recommendation by one of his brothers, who was the hotel's front-of-house manager. Just as in his early career, the latest move was courtesy of family connections. But it wouldn't have just been the good word that his brother put in for him that would have seen Cliveden eager to recruit Paul: his new bosses would no doubt see for themselves that he was destined for success, almost certainly backed up by impressive references from previous employers.

Once Paul took up his new role at Cliveden, he was soon to receive the ultimate seal of approval: from the Royal Family. As he went about his day job, focussed as ever, he discovered Queen Elizabeth, the Queen Mother would be visiting the hotel. Word of the impending visit came via his colleagues, heaping on the pressure to ensure his baking was even better than usual. And, it seems he well and truly rose to the challenge. Upon tasting one of Paul's scones, HM the Queen Mother was so impressed with its taste and texture that she made sure that her compliments were passed on to the chef. She went so far as to say that it was the best scone she had ever tasted. Not one of the best scones – *the* best. 'The Queen Mother called my scones the best in the world,' Paul told the

*Daily Mail* in another interview. It was thanks to his brother that the message was eventually passed on. 'I was working at Cliveden House and word reached me through my brother, who was one of the front-of-house managers,' he continued. Other reports suggest that the Queen Mum may even have entered the kitchen herself to pass on her praise in person. Regardless of how he came by the news, it was high praise indeed and an experience he has never forgotten.

In fact, Paul's scones may have been the reason why the Royal Family fell back in love with Cliveden. After changing ownership for years, it fell out of favour with Queen Victoria when purchased by Americans. And it seemed the Royals had all but turned their backs on Cliveden. That is, until the Queen Mother tasted Paul's scones! From then on they would regularly return to the house for important engagements and functions. Paul, understandably, was flattered by the compliment being paid him, while also finding it funny. 'The Royal Family had blackballed Cliveden for many years because Queen Victoria hated the fact that Americans – the Astors – had bought one of England's finest homes,' he explained to the *Daily Mail*. 'The Queen Mum was one of the first to come back. All because of my scones? Well, I think the setting had something to do with it.'

It's no mean feat that a boy from the Wirral had managed to eradicate years of antipathy from the UK's most powerful family, thanks to his baking skills. For him this was definitely a career hightlight and and it was fast becoming clear that he was destined for great things – despite still being in his early twenties. It's easy to imagine a certain buzz may have begun to surround his name in the world of high-end hotels and his reputation was starting to precede him. It would not be long before he moved on to yet another world-renowned hotel.

This time he took up an even bigger position at an even more prestigious hotel. Paul was recruited as the youngest-ever head baker at The Dorchester in London's Mayfair, taking up the role at the age of 24. It is listed as one of the best hotels in the world – and, yet again, it has an incredible history to boot. The Greenwich Mean Time website explains how the luxurious five-star first opened its doors on 18 April 1931. A gala luncheon was held to mark the occasion, with a guest list from the cream of society, including the Foreign Secretary Sir John Simon, Lord Halifax, the BBC's Lord Reith, Marchioness Curzon of Kedleston, the Earl of Rosebery and Margot, Countess of Oxford.

According to one commentator the 'colossal, pillarless Ballroom, with its mirrored walls set with sparkling studs, just as now, could accommodate a thousand in splendour'. And as such The Dorchester was immediately adopted for the grandest balls and parties of the elite – 'The Dorchester soon became synonymous with all that was most fashionable in British society'. By the end of the decade, two new banqueting rooms, the Holford Room and Orchid Room, and a new bar had been added. Meanwhile, the barman became something of legend for his dexterity with the cocktail shaker. Examples of his Martini, White Lady and Manhattan were sealed into the wall of the new bar for posterity, to be rediscovered during building work in 1979 – apparently as good as on the day they were mixed.

Over the years generations of artists and performers have bequeathed something of their own flamboyance. The Oliver Messel Suite was a particular favourite of both Noël Coward and Marlene Dietrich; though waspish about the paintwork, Cecil Beaton embraced the view. Both Judy Garland and Duke Ellington made The Dorchester their London base, while Somerset Maugham made a point of staying there for two or three months every year. In the 60s even the Beatles found it hard to resist. But it is actors who have always been most charmed by the glitz and glamour of The Dorchester: among them, Richard Burton and Elizabeth Taylor, James Mason, Charlton Heston, Yul Brynner, Julie Andrews, Warren Beatty, Peter Sellers, Tom Cruise, Nicole Kidman, Arnold Schwarzenegger and Kim Basinger.

And with Paul in charge of the whole baking operation at The Dorchester, he had reached the peak of his profession. Not only was he overseeing the whole department doing something he loved, he was doing so at what many perceive to be the finest hotel establishment in Britain. As such, he regards his time at The Dorchester as being the pinnacle of his career. The responsibilities would almost certainly have been wide-ranging, with every day posing new challenges and tasks for Paul and his team.

One advertisement published recently on the internet for the same role at a different, but equally prestigious, hotel chain outlined the responsibilities and essential job functions expected of a head baker. The head baker would report to the executive pastry chef, who would oversee the whole baking. First and foremost, Paul would be expected constantly to deliver the very best customer service for the guests staying at the hotel, meeting their every whim and expectation. In addition, there would be routine examinations of produce to ensure that pastries, cakes and bakes were always fresh and to the expected standard. On a daily basis he would be expected to oversee the preparation of breads, rolls, muffins and other baked goods according to standard recipes; also to inspect products for quality and consistency, during and after baking. He would be tasked to make sure the right quantity of baked goods was being prepared and there was enough stock in the storerooms to fulfil orders. He would also be responsible for maintaining a high level of cleanliness across all work areas, utensils and equipment. The buck would also stop with Paul – so before any baked items were delivered to guests he would have to check them over to ensure they were up to scratch. All that in the course of just one day – he would certainly have his work cut out for him!

Despite the gruelling schedule, Paul saw his time at the esteemed hotel as the epitome of everything he has achieved. 'I think I was at my peak when I was at The Dorchester,' he admitted to the *Radio Times*. It's a poignant comment, especially put in the context of the fact that he would go on to become one of Britain's biggest baking stars. But in true Hollywood style, he has kept his feet firmly on the ground. In the same interview, the journalist commented that he waved his hand around at the photo shoot, which included some of the best photographers and make-up artists in the business, as his publicist hovered nearby, and said: 'This [fame] is an illusion. It's not real, it's superficial.'

Perhaps there is one more story that might shed further light on why Paul was so enamoured with The Dorchester. This time he would be given the nod from another Royal: the Sultan of Brunei. The head of the oil-rich Arabic state would often stay at The Dorchester and, it appeared, he fell in love with one of Paul's creations – salmon brioche. 'During my time at The Dorchester Hotel in London, this brioche was a great favourite of the Sultan of Brunei,' he would later reveal alongside the recipe in one of his bestselling cookbooks. 'It's fabulous when toasted and served on a bed of rocket salad, with lemon and dill vinaigrette. You need to make the dough the day before.'

With praise from such exalted fans you might imagine that it would all go to Paul's head. Not so. He still remains the same down-to-earth character that he ever was, and says he finds it hard to come to terms with the fact that many people expect him to have changed. Also in his interview with the *Radio Times*, he said that he was sometimes reminded by his wife to take off the 'tracky bums' (tracksuit bottoms) before hitting the shops because he is now a celebrity. No matter how glamorous it may seem from the outside, celebrity and all its trappings is not, to his mind, so rewarding as making it at The Dorchester.

Despite working in some of the finest establishments in the world during the formative years of his career, Paul believes it's important that baking isn't seen as elite. While he may have baked for a number of Royals, he wants everyone to see the art of baking as accessible. 'Over the years I've been head baker at the Chester Grosvenor, The Dorchester and Cliveden, and I've baked for the Royal Family,' he told the *Sunday Express*, 'but now I want to get the nation baking. It's for everybody – it crosses gender and class. I come from the bottom of the industry, so if I like it, anybody will.'

It's fitting that his ethos is so focussed on opening up baking to everyone and anyone who wants to get involved. While he may have baked at some of Britain's finest establishments and for some of the world's most important people, baking shouldn't be seen as divisive. It's something that anyone can get involved in – and Paul's story proves just that. From humble beginnings he came to be the baker of choice for Royal families from around the world. 'My mum is very proud of me,' he admitted while talking to the *Radio Times*. But perhaps understandably, when Paul returns home it seems people treat him differently, maybe a little overcome by his success. 'Back home I go into a pub, and people stare at you for a long period of time. Which up north is a sign of aggression,' he has revealed.

Regardless of this, Paul will always know that his baking was fit for a King... or rather, a Queen Mother and a Sultan. And let's be honest, how many people can say that?

# CHAPTER 4

# Six Years in Cyprus

After establishing himself as one of the best bakers in Britain's hotel business, Paul had already achieved what might have seemed an impossible task as a young boy growing up in the Wirral. After reaching the pinnacle of his profession as head baker at The Dorchester, arguably one of the world's finest hotels, it would have been easy for him to rest on his laurels. After all, where do you go from there? By now he was in his late 20s, and had dedicated all of his formative years to his trade. But Paul being Paul, he was ready for a fresh challenge and a chance to spread his wings. Very soon the opportunity would present itself to do just that, but it would mean leaving Britain.

For it seemed that Paul's reputation had spread across the globe and his credentials had come to the attention of the Cypriot Foreign Minister. It was around 1994 when Alekos

Michaelides first heard of Paul and it just so happened that he was looking to recruit a baker to work at some of his luxury five-star hotels on the sunshine isle. These prestigious establishments have long been a retreat for holidaymakers from across Europe, courtesy of the fact that the island's eastern Mediterranean location enjoys a summer climate eight months of the year. The Foreign Minister, alongside his political duties, also happened to own a string of hotels. Not only did he want someone to come and bake exquisite bread for his guests, but also to train the other bakers.

Curious as to what the opportunity might hold, Paul decided to travel out to the island for a few days to meet the hotel owners and find out what the job might actually entail. Little did he realise this was a trip that would change his life forever. 'I flew out for an interview thinking it would just be a jolly for two days but came back really wanting to work there, which was so different to my normal character,' he explained in an interview with the *Daily Mail*. Having spent most of his life in the UK and rarely venturing abroad, naturally he felt comfortable in Britain and regarded it as his home. This was probably compounded by the success of his professional life. But when Paul was offered the job, somehow he knew it was right. Perhaps it was a gut instinct, or maybe just a desire for a change of scenery, nevertheless he jumped at the opportunity and moved to Cyprus. Initially he was offered a year's contract but in reality he ended up staying there until 2000. 'I'd always been such a home bird,' he told the *Daily Mail*. 'When I moved to Cyprus, Mum gave it three weeks – I stayed for six years.'

Paul's job was based at the Anassa Hotel in Paphos, as well

as the Annabelle Hotel in nearby Latchi, a working fishing harbour and peaceful family holiday destination on the northwest coast. The brief was a simple one – teaching the Cypriot members of the kitchen staff how to bake European-style. That meant everything from afternoon teas to cupcakes, as well as brioches, pains au chocolat and croissants. Both hotels are part of the Thanos Luxury Hotels group. They had cultivated a reputation for being among the best hotels in that part of the world, and so it was a huge compliment to Paul that he was given such a senior position. As well as the Anassa and Annabelle hotels, the Thanos Luxury Hotels group also includes the Almyra, a five-star beachfront property. Paul would doubtless have felt at home with the company because it was – and still is – a family-run firm.

All the hotels in the group had everything you might expect of five-star luxury – sprawling grounds and incredible swimming pools, attentive staff who would stop at nothing to make the guests feel welcome, as well as beautiful beach-side settings overlooking the crystal-clear waters of the Mediterranean. According to the company website, the Anassa Hotel was considered 'the jewel in Cyprus's crown – a majestic year-round resort that exudes the charm of a traditional Cypriot village'. Indeed, the name itself means 'queen' in ancient Greek. On arrival Paul would almost certainly have been swept away by the setting, for this was truly something else. Tumbling down a secluded hillside towards the infinite blue of the eastern Mediterranean, the resort's classical low-rise buildings and tropical gardens are arranged around an idyllic village square complete with

Byzantine chapel. Set in an area of outstanding natural beauty, the facilities are inspired by the surrounding landscape: from the extensive Thalassotherapy programme in the luxury Roman-style Thalassa Spa to local, seasonal produce served in a choice of five 'farm-fresh' restaurants. As well as kids' clubs and beach activities, the hotel had various five-star silver services, where Paul's baking expertise would have been put to great use. In addition, there were boutiques and hotel gardens for guests to while away the hours.

Meanwhile, at the other hotel in the chain where Paul would be working, the Annabelle, the vibe could perhaps be considered less grand and more chilled out. Sitting on the Paphos waterfront, 'its cool, peaceful interiors, understated design and warm, caring service combine to create a distinct atmosphere of unpretentious elegance', according to the hotel website. There are four restaurants and five bars that 'showcase seasonal produce, delicate local wines and traditional Cypriot charm, with live music at the hotel almost every night of the week'. Additionally, 'glittering waterfalls reflect the tantalising blue of the Mediterranean; swaying palms slow life to a blissful pace'.

Of course the level of hospitality and service by now came as second nature to Paul. However, what was different this time was the fact that he was at one of Europe's premier holiday destinations. The main attraction of Paphos is the subtropical climate. Here, the summer season stretches from April to November, making it particularly appealing to sunseekers. Paphos enjoys the mildest temperatures of the whole of Cyprus, reaching 20°C even during the winter months.

What's more, Paphos is steeped in a romantic history, being the mythical birthplace of Aphrodite, the Greek goddess of love and beauty, and where she apparently rose from the sea. As such, Old Paphos became the most famous and important place for worshipping Aphrodite in the ancient world; in Greco-Roman times it was also Cyprus's capital city, housing the Roman Governor's palace, the remains of which are still a leading tourist attraction. In the early 1970s it experienced enormous economic growth, along with a massive expansion in infrastructure and building to turn Paphos into the tourist metropolis that it is today. This came about when the Cypriot government decided to invest heavily in new technologies to regenerate the area. The scheme included splashing out thousands upon thousands of Cypriot pounds on irrigation dams, as well as water distribution works, road infrastructure and making Paphos a true hub for transport, thanks to the building of Paphos International Airport, which welcomed hundreds of flights a day during the peak season. During the 1980s and 90s regeneration of the whole area continued, with an increasing number of hotels, restaurants and bars available for tourists to enjoy. Suddenly Paphos was one of *the* most popular tourist hot spots in the whole of Europe.

Nowadays this remains the case, not least because of all the special deals that are available from tour operators. Paphos's present-day population, as of 2011, was just under 33,000, and the resort that stands there today is built around a medieval port and fishing harbour. It was certainly a world away from the Wirral. The climate, crystal-blue waters and the exotic culture were all alien to Paul, but proved an incredible new experience as he took up an exciting phase in his career. And as he set about dispensing baking wisdom to his colleagues, he quickly settled into the Cypriot pace of life too.

'I went to Cyprus on a year's contract as a baker in the Anassa and Annabelle Resorts but ended up staying six years,' he told the *Sunday Express*. 'I was there to teach Cypriots European-style baking – croissants, Danish pastries, breads – and I was living the life out there.'

But despite throwing himself into his new job, Paul has since admitted that he came close to quitting to retrain as a chef. After all, having spent the best part of his teens and 20s working in some of the finest establishments, what else was left for him to achieve in his chosen field? But luckily for the thousands of devotees who would later read every word of his cookbooks and follow his TV shows, this initial hesitation over whether or not to continue as a baker proved short-lived. 'Because I'd been at the top of my profession there was no one to learn from and it was hard to stay motivated,' he explained in an interview with the *Daily Mail*. 'I had to teach myself by reading books and travelling.' But for Paul, who was never academically gifted (he had, after all, chosen to pursue a course in sculpture over traditional subjects), all the extra studying seemed daunting. Perhaps understandably, he swiftly came to the conclusion that he should stick to what he did best – baking.

So when Paul was offered a contract with the Cypriot hotel chain, he readily signed on the dotted line and didn't look back. But if he had thought that working abroad with sun and sea on tap would be a breeze, he could think again. The demands of his job were tough and he was expected to deliver an enormous quota of baked products every single day. In an interview with the *Daily Mail* given some years after returning from the island, he admitted that he was 'haunted' by having to bake a staggering 500 lavroches – a special type of local sesame seed bread enjoyed by the Cypriots – not every week, not every month but every single day! Despite a wealth of experience, he was still on a steep learning curve and later revealed that part of what he loved about his stint in Cyprus was the fact that he got to learn so much more about baking – in particular, foreign baking.

Paul relished the chance to explore the history and international traditions of bread-making in particular – something that he would re-visit in a big way when, years later, he would present his own series on the BBC titled *Paul Hollywood's Bread*. His time in Cyprus would forever influence the way he saw cooking, giving him a completely different perspective on an art form that he felt he had already mastered. 'I lived in Cyprus for many years and travelled through the Middle East,' he told the *Independent* newspaper. 'So I learnt that you can stuff a pitta with salads, meats and herbs and have the freshest, tastiest meal ever. I love the way the Italians use their stale bread up as well, as bruschetta or covered in crushed garlic and olive oil, torn into pieces and tossed in a salad with capers, anchovies, onion and crisp lettuce.'

But he was particularly keen to get the Cypriot traditional flatbread down to a fine art – to the extent that many of his followers now say he has developed the ultimate easy-to-bake recipe, as witnessed in the cookbooks he has gone on to publish. Experts and novices alike say his recipes for pittas and wraps are also seen as simple and to the point, being easy to master in a standard home kitchen, but giving an authentic, tasty result too. It's not so much in the preparation or the ingredients, but the way in which they are baked, Paul insists. 'I lived in Cyprus for six years where I learnt all about flatbreads,' he revealed in an interview with the *Daily Telegraph*. 'The secret is all about temperature.'

So after toying with the idea of possibly turning his back on baking, it seemed Cyprus had reignited his love affair with baking. There, he was exposed to so many different types of baked products and a variety of methodologies. However, while Paul managed significantly to improve his oeuvre, it does seem that perfection might elude him when it comes to certain recipes. In particular, he pinpoints a bread called Flaouna. It's a local bread famously enjoyed on the island as part of the Easter festivities but usually made and consumed by Orthodox Greeks. Pastry is filled with cheese and occasionally raisins are injected into the dough mix before the breads are sprinkled with sesame seeds to finish. Flaouna was to become a recipe that Paul would regularly reproduce in years to come. The time spent in Cyprus would not only change his life, but influence his baking too.

Aside from learning wonderful new ways with baking to keep himself – and the hotel guests – entertained, Paul also developed other interests while in Cyprus. In particular, he liked biking. Not just any biking, but superbiking. It's a sport that has become big news around the world, though not especially in the UK. While rules vary from series to series, in general the motorcycles must maintain the same profile as their road-going counterparts, with the same overall appearance as seen from the front, rear and sides. In addition, the frame cannot be modified. Teams may modify some elements of the bike, including the suspensions, brakes and the diameter and size of wheel. Generally superbike motorcycles must have four-stroke engines of between 850 and 1200cc for twins, and between 750 and 1000cc for four-cylinder machines.

Whether Paul was looking for a way to let off steam after his long days working at the hotels, or whether he was simply trying out a new sport, he admits he fell in love with superbiking. During his free time he and his friends would potter down to the local RAF base, where the wide-open concrete spaces were ideal for the fast pace of the bikes. 'I had a big superbike and I used to race it on the runway at RAF Akrotiri. The police were employed to work out who was fastest over a quarter-mile drag, using their radar guns. I had the fastest bike in Cyprus in '98. Great fun,' he told the *Sunday Express*. But he also admits that the sport saw him experience – perhaps – too close a brush with the Law. On more than one occasion, he used to race past the cops at incredibly fast speeds. 'I used to race my bike at 200mph past the police,' he admitted in an interview with the *Daily Mail*.

And if that wasn't enough to satisfy his adrenaline junkie ways, he also developed an interest in other adventurous, fast-paced hobbies while on the island. 'Not a lot of people know this but I'm very good at go-karting. I lived in Cyprus from 1994 to 2000 and used to go-kart every day,' he told the *Sunday Express*. 'My weakness is cakes and cars. If I see a nice car, I've got to get into it.' Meanwhile, if he wasn't propelling himself horizontally in a go-kart or superbike, Paul also liked to take the plunge on daring trips across waterfalls. 'The bravest thing I've ever done is jump off a waterfall in Cyprus when I was 30,' he also told the *Sunday Express*. 'I'd heard that people had done it, so I wanted to try. I was petrified but I did it.' So if he wasn't getting his adrenaline fix through tight deadlines in the kitchen, he certainly managed to do so thanks to his love of sport.

And it was one such action-packed sport that would eventually lead him to one of the most important moments of his life. Along with other hobbies, he also took up scuba diving and would regularly take lessons in the mornings. After spending the first few years of his career getting up long before sunrise, in Cyprus the bulk of Paul's work would be in the afternoons and evenings, leaving the mornings free. And it was through scuba diving that he would come to meet his future wife Alexandra – or 'Alex' as he calls her. British-born Alexandra had also left the UK for a new life in Cyprus. Born in Kent and the middle of three kids, Alexandra had been educated in a private Ursaline convent. Her father, Michael Moores, who died 20 years ago from a heart attack, was an executive in a construction firm. Her mother Gloria, who was half-French and half-Norwegian, worked on the international newsdesk of the BBC. After her happy upbringing, Alexandra wanted an adventure and, so, decamped to Cyprus. As a

PADI-qualified diving instructor, she soon found a job teaching locals and holidaymakers how they too could enjoy the beautiful waters that surround Cyprus. It seemed only fitting that the pair would hit it off. After all, according to ancient tradition Aphrodite, goddess of love and fertility, was born from the waves off the coast of Cyprus and appeared to cast her spell over the couple. Paul was one of Alexandra's students and instantly smitten.

Perhaps somewhat inevitably he used his skills in the kitchen to attract her attention. In an interview with the *Daily Mail*, he said: 'I used to bring her Danish pastries and her favourite had champagne ganache in it and orange segments on the top.' Who could possibly say no? Certainly not Alexandra, it seemed. 'I wooed her with food,' he admitted.

For her part, 32-year-old Alexandra was bowled over by Paul's charm and cooking skills. 'He was a fantastic looking guy. He was absolutely lovely with piercing blue eyes and I thought: "Wow!"' said Alexandra in a later interview with the *Daily Mail*. 'I didn't even look at the bread. We fell in love very quickly. Two weeks was all it took – we both knew. Paul was lovely, he made me the most wonderful pastries for breakfast. Show me a woman who doesn't like chocolate!'

But while Paul was a master baker in the kitchen and impressed Alexandra with his culinary skills, it appeared that she too was a dab hand when it came to cooking. According to him, it just so happened that they shared a love of food. And while Alexandra didn't cook by trade when they met, it was something she loved to throw herself into when she wasn't teaching scuba. 'She does all the cooking at home,'

Paul said in one interview. And she had put those culinary skills to the test while running hotels in the France during ski seasons. 'She used to run chalets in the Alps and was a resort manager. In fact, she should be on the telly herself.'

Alexandra says it was her mother Gloria who had encouraged her to try out cooking as a hobby. 'My mother was desperately keen for me to go off to university, but I had other ideas,' Alexandra said in an interview with the *Daily Mail*. 'After school, I did a secretarial course, just to please her, because she hoped that I'd go on to marry a nice diplomat, doctor or dentist, but I'm afraid that I took off travelling instead.'

Paul remembers the beginning of their relationship fondly and admits matters progressed very quickly as the couple fell head over heels in love. Things went so well that within three months he had proposed and a year later they were married. 'I had a villa and a Suzuki superbike, and took up diving,' he said in one interview. 'I'd come back from work, get the scuba kit and go wreck or tunnel diving. Alex was a diving instructor and I met her in the water. I asked her to marry me three months after we started dating.' It's easy to imagine how the romance would have blossomed against the backdrop of the paradise island, and very soon they were planning their nuptials – in true Cypriot style.

When it came to the wedding day, this was no quiet affair. Understandably, Paul remembers that day as one of the most important landmarks in his life, a day he will never forget. The ceremony took place on 11 September 1998, almost four years after he had moved to the island. 'The best day of my life was the day I got married in 1998,' he told the *Sunday Express*. 'We had our reception at Viklari, an open-air restaurant in Cyprus. It was full of our Cypriot friends and we came back to a bed covered with money, because that's the tradition.' In the same interview he shared a photo of the magical day. Describing the snap, which obviously holds a special place in his heart, he said: 'This is my wedding day. Alex and I got married on 11 September 1998, in the oldest Christian church in the world in Paphos, Cyprus. It was boiling hot – 42°C – and I'm a lot darker and slimmer in the photo. With my black hair and unfeasible tan, I look Italian or Greek.'

It was obviously a momentous occasion for both Paul and Alexandra. A few years later in October 2001 they would have a son, whom they called Joshua (Josh), but only after they returned to the UK. For the time being though, the pair enjoyed being newlyweds – in particular, exploring their shared love of good food and wine. 'My perfect evening is a meal out with my wife with a nice bottle of wine,' Paul later told the *Sunday Express*. There was one special restaurant – Paradise – where the couple would always dine whenever their work schedules allowed. 'We'd have lobster and chips at a restaurant we used to go to in Cyprus called Paradise,' Paul said. In truth, it seemed as though their life in Cyprus was pretty much close to paradise.

But after four or five years on the island and just before he and Alexandra married, Paul had started to get itchy feet. It seemed he was ready for something new. 'After four or five years, when I felt I'd learned enough, I did my own thing,' he said in one interview with the *Sunday Express*. But just as he began to feel restless and as though he needed a new challenge, it presented itself in the form of television work.

It was the second time that Paul had appeared on screen, having already featured on his local news show while working at the Chester Grosvenor. On this occasion, a TV crew from the UK had arrived on Cyprus and were desperate for someone with a good command of English to help film a segment about Greek baking. Alongside her work as a scuba-diving instructor, Alexandra was also doing PR for the hotel where Paul worked. The crew asked if she knew of any possible people they might film, and of course Alexandra immediately suggested Paul would be perfect for the job. As he explained to the *Sunday Express*: 'It was in Cyprus, just before Alex and I married, that I started doing telly.' A British film crew came over to the hotel for a programme called *Food from the Village*. By now Alex was doing PR for the hotel in her role as the guest relations manager. Alexandra had previous experience of working in the PR trade, representing luxury goods firm Loewe and the fashion range Nicole Farhi in London. She spoke to the crew who said they wanted to make a programme about Cypriot food and baking. They asked Alexandra if she could put them in touch with some local people to help them.

In an interview with the *Daily Mail*, Alexandra remembers how she told the crew they should forget trying to hire someone local, and use Paul instead. 'I said: "No, no, no. The person you need to see is Paul." Because Paul is so gregarious, he knows everything,' Alexandra recounted. 'If there's a good place to eat, he will know it. Even our Cypriot friends would say: "How does he know this? He knows things about Cyprus we don't know." So I set up a meeting with the TV company and they loved Paul. They put him in front of a camera and you could just see how brilliant he was. He dominated the screen. After they had finished filming, the production team said to me: "He needs to go back to the UK and get an agent."' Paul took to it like a duck to water. It was immediate. 'One day I saw a newspaper article about Jamie Oliver after *The Naked Chef* had started on TV and I said to Paul, "You could do that." I just knew that one day he would end up as big as the celebrity chefs. Always, always I knew it. I believed in him completely because he was so good.'

But Paul wasn't so sure. The renowned food critic Thane Prince was involved in the project. Thane wrote for the *Daily Telegraph* for some 12 years, on top of writing a dozen books, and ran the world-famous Aldeburgh Cookery School on the Suffolk coast. She and the project director were very impressed with Paul's work on screen: with his good looks, easy charm and natural aptitude for baking, he seemed a natural in front of the camera. 'The crew asked me to do something to camera – I'd never done anything like that before,' he recalled. 'The director said I should work in TV. I thought, "Yeah, right!"'

While he may have been flippant to begin with, it appeared that TV would be the new challenge he had been waiting for. After all, it would be a way for him to get his name out there and for an even wider audience to get to know him and his recipes. After this taste of what it might be like to be a TV star, he and Alexandra decided it was time for a new beginning and they made plans to return to the UK and settle down back in Blighty.

And now as Paul returned to home shores, he decided it really was time to give his TV career a kick-start, and so he took the necessary steps to try and transform himself into a television chef.

# CHAPTER 5

# Back in Blighty

It was 2000 and the Hollywoods had decided to return to the UK. It's fair to say Paul had achieved all he could possibly achieve in the six years that he had been away from his home country. Not only had he excelled at working at one of the best hotel chains in the world, but, perhaps more importantly, he had also met the love of his life in Alexandra. Perhaps he felt that after settling down, it was time to return to the UK and put down some firm roots in the place he knew so well.

But once back in Britain, something was niggling away at Paul as a possible career move. Having done a small amount of TV work in Cyprus, thanks in no small part to Alexandra's excellent PR skills, it seemed he might have caught the bug. Now he was curious to explore his chances as a TV chef and so he decided that it was time to sign up for something that all would-be TV stars have: an agent. Paul has freely admitted that the little bit of TV work in Cyprus meant that he could forge a career on the small screen. 'When I left Cyprus, people asked why I was going. I thought that when you'd been offered TV, you go off and make loads of money,' he admitted in an interview with the *Sunday Express*. Naturally it would be a dream come true if he could make the transition from a hotel chef – albeit a highly successful one – to a TV personality with the power to promote his love of baking. Not least it would be well paid, but this would also be a way for him to convey his passion to a much wider audience.

It was the late 90s and daytime cookery shows had suddenly become hugely popular. On the BBC in particular there were two regular shows that did well in audience viewer ratings – *Ready Steady Cook* and *Can't Cook Won't Cook*. Both had very simple formats. The first of these two shows – *Ready Steady Cook* – worked as follows. Two members of the public – although in later episodes this changed to celebrities – would bring along a set of ingredients worth no more than £5 for two celebrity chefs to conjure up a dish (or dishes) during the course of the show. The challenge was to come up with something original and appetising, all for a fraction of the price they might be used to. The two celebrity chef teams were called 'red tomato' and 'green pepper' – although this was later changed to the 'red kitchen' and the 'green kitchen' after a revamp of the show in 2007. Neither chef would have any idea what would be in the ingredients bags before they were unveiled during filming, so the name of the game was quick thinking and original recipes!

The original *Ready Steady Cook* series aired on BBC2, although celebrity specials were screened on BBC1, with the show itself first hosted by telly favourite Fern Britton between the launch in 1994 and 2000, before her duties were taken over by Ainsley Harriott, one of the most flamboyant, charismatic celebrity chefs ever, who used to cook on the show itself before emerging as a star in his own right in 2000. He continued presenting *Ready Steady Cook* until the series was finally cancelled in 2010 after a staggering and impressive 16 years.

The other of the two shows, *Can't Cook Won't Cook*, hit the screens a year after *Ready Steady Cook*'s debut, in 1995. Whereas *Ready Steady Cook* would be an evening show, *Can't Cook Won't Cook* was to be broadcast on BBC1 on weekday mornings, usually after the breakfast news. The format was similar, but different: two would-be cooks were nominated by friends or family to come on the show in order to be guided by a world-class chef on how to prepare a meal. As the title of the show suggests, neither was particularly keen on getting their hands dirty in the kitchen, however. The first contestant was meant to be inept and lacking the knowledge about how to cook, while the second had the ability but refused – because they were too busy, just too lazy or disinclined to do so! After both teams had completed preparing their meals the nominator would be blindfolded and instructed to taste the food and deliver an opinion. Following this they would decide whose dish was best, and in the event of a tie, the chef would choose which dish came out on top. A prize – usually something along the lines of a food blender or other kitchen gadget, which would hopefully inspire the winner to develop their cooking talents – was awarded to the winner. That show ran for a total of five series until 2000, when it was cancelled after a total of 685 episodes.

Despite the runaway success of both shows, Paul was unaware of either series – not least because they weren't broadcast in Cyprus and he had certainly not kept tabs on what was in or out while he was away. 'When I returned in 1999, I signed with an agent,' he explained in an interview with the *Sunday Express*. 'I had a call a week later saying, "Would you like to do a series called *Use Your Loaf* with James Martin?" I said, "Who the hell is James Martin?" I'd been in Cyprus – I didn't know about *Ready Steady Cook*.'

It seemed there was a snag in his plan. In all the time Paul had been away, suddenly these shows, in which he might easily have participated, had become hits. How would he ever become a TV chef if he didn't understand the big success stories? Luckily it was James Martin himself who would help make Paul a TV star.

James had become a regular on the *Ready Steady Cook* team, propelling him to household name status across Britain. English chef James first appeared on TV just three years before Paul returned from Cyprus, in 1996. Born in 1972, in Malton, in Yorkshire's North Riding, Martin came from a family of farmers. He had developed a love of food and cooking after spending his formative years helping his mother in and around the kitchen. At school, he didn't excel at academic subjects. Although committed and hard-working, he suffered undiagnosed dyslexia, which caused difficulties, but his passion and love for cooking carried him through.

On leaving school, he decided to enrol in a catering class at Scarborough Technical College, near to where he lived. And while school had always been a slog, he flourished at the college, and he has often been described in press reports as the 'star pupil'. His big moment came during his final exams. The college had recruited the top celebrity chef and restaurateur Antony Worrall Thompson to come and judge his final exam. Worrall Thompson was so impressed that he immediately offered him a job. He recruited the northern lad to come and work at his prestigious One Ninety Queen's Gate restaurant in Kensington, west London. After cutting his teeth there he moved on to the Windsor branch of their well-respected hotel chain, Hotel du Vin, where he took over as head chef. The hotel chain has 14 establishments around the UK, including city-centre locations such as Newcastle and London, and townhouses in some of the UK's most charming towns, like Tunbridge Wells and Cheltenham.

But by 1996, James had been headhunted to do TV work. His first project was in a show that revolved around Yorkshire cuisine – something he knew a lot about. It was called *James Martin: Yorkshire's Finest*, and was set in various locations across the sprawling county with a distinct emphasis on – yep, you've guessed it, Yorkshire cuisine. But it would be on *Ready Steady Cook* that James would come to prominence and truly become a household name as he quickly rose to become one of the most popular chefs on the show. A combination of his cheeky-chappy personality, his good manners and quick thinking when it came to coming up with recipes, made him a firm favourite with the viewers. After nine years on the show he was then given his own series, *Saturday Kitchen* – a topical magazine show that aired on BBC1 once a week on a Saturday as the name suggests and focussed on food that James would cook with the help of celebrity guests. It hit record viewing figures of 2.1 million. Other shows he has added to his CV over the years include *Sweet Baby James* and *The Great British Village Show*. Like numerous big names on daytime TV, in autumn 2006 James was asked to take part in the successful BBC1 ballroom dancing competition, *Strictly Come Dancing*. He proved so popular that he eventually reached the semi-finals of the series before bowing out with his professional dance partner, Camilla Dallerup.

But there was something else that James would do that would become a memorable highlight of his career: he would also work with Paul on one show and it would end with them becoming firm friends. When Paul returned to the UK in 1999 and was on the lookout for more TV work, he would see his path cross with this star on the rise. Alongside *Ready Steady Cook*, James had been offered the chance to front a show called *Use Your Loaf*. Paul's reputation as a master baker ensured he was seen as a perfect partner to James. The show's format is described on the Good Food Channel's website as the pair 'teaming up for an unforgettable journey into the world of posh breads and baking'. The website continues: 'The pair set out to prove that there's more to bread than the simple loaves available in your local supermarket. The light-hearted series looks at such easy and imaginative delicacies as Greek bread and dips, scones and delicious pastries like choux'. In each episode the two TV chefs were joined by an expert guest who would sample and then critique their creations. As the website concludes: 'It's time to forget about plain white sliced, let Paul and James rise to the occasion. They've got a lot to "prove".'

In fairness, the show itself didn't make a huge impact with viewers, although it continues to be repeated today – perhaps partly because of Paul's more recent success and James's enduring appeal as a stalwart of the TV cooking scene. It seemed that Paul was not to become a TV star overnight. As he himself conceded years later in an interview with the *Sunday Express*: 'I expected to be the next Jamie Oliver. It didn't happen.' His blunt admission gives an insight into the harsh realities of how hard it is to make it in the world of TV: while you may be picked to front a show, it doesn't mean that it will necessarily lead to long and lasting success. Unfortunately for Paul, at this juncture in his career it didn't look as if TV stardom was coming his way and the regular on-screen work seemed to dry up, at least for the foreseeable future. As we now know, he would later find huge success on *The Great British Bake Off*, but for the time being he had to put those aspirations on the back burner. In fact, he would soon develop some business interests that would allow him to become the boss of his own company, doing what he loved.

One good thing that came out of the whole process was his closeness to James. Paul remembers vividly their first meeting. The pair hit it off instantly, not least because of their shared love of food and drink – even if it was of the fast food variety as opposed to haute cuisine. 'I went, "Who's James Martin?" because I'd been out of the country six years,' Paul explained to the *Daily Mail*. 'I met him in London's Met Bar and we had a great chat about cars. As the night progressed we went for some fast food. I've never seen anyone eat a bucket of chicken so quick.'

From here on, a friendship quickly blossomed and it got to the stage where James would often spend the night at Paul's house. 'James used to stay at mine a lot,' recalled Paul in one interview with the *Daily Mail*. There is one amusing anecdote that Paul, to this day, shares about how James and his mother Gill both stayed with him on the same night. Now it's important to remember that James was fast becoming a big star on daytime TV. While it might be easy to assume that nowadays Paul is the bigger star, thanks to the *Bake Off* franchise, at the time James was more in demand as a TV personality. So, in the morning, when Paul's mum and James sat around the breakfast table, she found it highly amusing that she had slept in close proximity to someone so famous. 'The first time he came down for breakfast my mum was there, fully made up, and when he left she went, "I can't believe it – James Martin was sleeping on top of me last night!"' said Paul in the same interview.

'She meant the room above. She had photographs taken with him and built a shrine on the mantelpiece, demoting the photos of me, my wife and son to the top of the DVD player.'

No doubt Mrs Hollywood had no idea at the time that her son would go on to become an equally, perhaps arguably more, successful TV star. His time would come eventually.

But while Paul's TV career wasn't exactly taking off in 1999, it seemed like the perfect opportunity for him to put down some roots. After tying the knot in Cyprus in 1998, it was perhaps the natural step for Alexandra and Paul to start a family. The couple were also thrilled to discover Alexandra was pregnant. But sadly, to begin with, it wasn't to be.

'We were so thrilled, incredibly so, because we wanted children, but unfortunately the pregnancy was ectopic,' Alexandra revealed in an interview with the *Daily Mail*. 'You think, "Ooh, isn't it wonderful, I'm pregnant," and then it all goes horribly wrong. We'd had this big move and it was all quite dreadful. We'd just got back to the UK and I felt so ill. I'd always been very healthy, but my skin looked like porridge. I started having these dreadful pains, but I kept telling myself: "Perhaps this is normal." You go into denial. You know something is wrong, but you don't want to acknowledge it because it should be such a happy time.'

Alexandra remembers the night it all went wrong vividly. 'One evening the pains were particularly bad, and I said to Paul, "I need to go to hospital now,"' she told the *Daily Mail*. He whizzed me into hospital and they discovered the pregnancy was developing in one of my fallopian tubes. I had to have emergency surgery, and it was such a huge thing to take on board. You think you have this wonderful, happy moment to look forward to – our first baby – and then it all goes pear-shaped. Not only that, but I had complications and was told I might find it very difficult to get pregnant again. My chances had been halved, but Paul was a huge support.'

But luckily, eight months later in Spring 2001, Alexandra got some welcome news – she was pregnant again. '[Paul] was always confident we would have children,' Alexandra told the

*Daily Mail*, 'and amazingly eight months later I fell pregnant with Joshua. When I did the pregnancy test, I waved the stick under Paul's nose and he was so pleased, incredibly so, big grin from ear to ear. I didn't mind what I had, as long as the baby was healthy, but Paul dreamed of having a son.'

The pregnancy was by no means easy, though. And that, understandably, put Alexandra on edge. 'For the first three months I felt sick all the time. It was like being locked on a ship in high seas,' she told the *Daily Mail*. 'I was very anaemic with low blood sugar, so I would send out Paul to buy pink French fancies – disgusting things – so you can imagine how he felt about that. 'He used to say, "I will make you this, I will make you that" and I'd reply: "No, it has to be bright pink French fancies." I haven't touched them since.'

In October 2001 Alexandra went into labour and Paul was by Alexandra's side during the 18-hour labour. She couldn't eat, but he was popular with the medical staff, who happily polished off all the home-made cakes he brought into the hospital. 'Paul cried when Joshua was born,' Alexandra said to the *Daily Mail*. 'He was so happy and from day one he was a brilliant daddy. We  would have liked more children, but sadly it just didn't happen.'

When it came to the little boy's christening there was only one person whom Paul wanted as godfather – his close friend James Martin. And as he grew up, it seemed that Joshua too would develop a keen interest in baking. No doubt it would have been a touching and emotional moment for Paul when he first baked a cake or whipped up a dessert with the help of his son, not least because it probably reminded him that history was repeating itself. Paul has often spoken about how his love of bakery was born out of the fact that he would be surrounded by his parents cooking up sweet treats in the kitchen as he grew up. And, of course, Paul first got a taste for working in the baking industry thanks to the leg-up his own father gave him, when he employed him behind the counter at his bakeries across England. Now, Joshua too was developing a keen interest for doing exactly the same thing. In one interview with the *Daily Mail*, Paul revealed how even young Josh has his views on his dad's baking: 'I made a chocolate roulade with him the other day and as we were about to put the cream filling in he stopped me and said we needed to add fruit as it was too sweet! He loves to challenge my recipes. He's got quite mature taste and complains if I try to feed him a plain white baguette so I have to make him a sourdough instead.' With Paul as his father, and James Martin as his godfather, it's easy to imagine that Joshua may well end up following a culinary career as he gets older.

And it seems that Paul's somewhat opinionated views when it comes to baking and enjoying food would eventually rub off on his son. 'Josh knows his food and what he likes and doesn't like,' Paul told the *Sunday People*. And it wasn't just at home that Josh started to air his views on what tasted good – and what wasn't so good. Paul continued: 'He started criticising the food at school – much to the dinner ladies' dismay – so now he takes a packed lunch every day, which solves the problem.' No doubt Paul may have secretly approved of the fact that his offspring had inherited his discerning taste buds!

But Paul and Josh weren't the only members of the

Hollywood family with a passion for good food, it seemed. Alexandra was also giving her husband a run for his money in the kitchen, and Paul has previously admitted in interviews to being constantly impressed with the dishes she created in the family kitchen. While he may have gone on to become a tough-talking TV judge on *The Great British Bake Off*, known for his acerbic comments and blunt criticisms, Alexandra was the one person who didn't receive any such criticism. 'Alexandra is an unbelievably good chef,' Paul enthused in the same interview with the *Sunday People*. 'I've never felt like I had to bite my tongue and say something is nice when it isn't,' he continued. 'She makes a great risotto or steak.' It seemed a match made in heaven. 'In our house I'm happy for her to cook while I get on with the baking,' he added.

And while family life itself couldn't be more perfect, it seemed, it was around this time that he and Alexandra decided to set up home in the picturesque county of Kent. Although originally from the northwest, Paul chose to set down roots further south. With mile upon mile of lush countryside, orchards and allotments, Kent is best known as the 'Garden of England'. In the end, the Hollywoods settled on the small and pretty village of Wingham, which is positioned on the ancient coastal road near Canterbury.

Local history states that Wingham has existed since the Stone Age, although it was only acknowledged as a village during the Roman period. According to the Domesday Book, the manor house in Wingham was owned by the then Archbishop of Canterbury but the village was really put on the map when the Archbishop of Peckham opened a college there in the 1280s. One of the village pubs still popular with locals today – the Red Lion Inn – has also been there since the 1200s and doubtless would have been somewhere that Paul and Alexandra may have socialised with friends over the years that they lived in Wingham. As well as the Red Lion, there are two other hostelries called the Anchor and the Dog. St Mary the Virgin church dates from the early thirteenth century, with fabric dating back to the Norman and Victorian eras. Nowadays Wingham is a small, pretty village with good connections to other towns such as Sandwich and Canterbury.

It's easy to see why Paul would want to settle there with his family. Not only was the village in a beautiful part of the country, but it also allowed easy access to London from the nearby train stations of Adisham and Aylesham. It was a hub for industry during the early 1900s, after the now infamous East Kent Light Railway was constructed between 1911 and 1917 in order to service coal mines opening up in the area around that period. The Wingham Colliery station was opened, along with the Wingham Canterbury Road and Wingham Town. However, Wingham Colliery never opened for production and the line failed; it was completely closed to passengers in 1948, with the section north of Eythorne closed to freight in 1951. Plans and some advanced earthworks had been commenced in the 1920s to extend the line from Wingham Canterbury Road station to Canterbury via Stodmarsh.

Once Paul and Alexandra had settled on Wingham, they now needed to find a home. Eventually they chose The Old

Canonry, which dates back at least to 1286 (the date over the door), although it may well be older than that. It is so historic and important a building that the *Sunday Telegraph* newspaper dedicated a whole feature to it in 2006. Period property expert Clive Aslet described it as 'not just a house, it's part of history.' He went on to say:

In the basement is a section of what could be Roman road. Over time the road outside was built up to leave the original surface several feet underground. The oldest houses in Britain are built of stone. A handful exist from the late twelfth century. The oldest above-ground part of The Old Canonry dates from the late thirteenth century, when the College of St Mary was founded by the Archbishop of Canterbury. Earlier wooden houses rested directly on the soil, with no regard for the rot that would plague later occupants, but the timbers of The Old Canonry sit on a flint wall.

Key characteristics include thick stone walls, small windows, half timbering and a crown post roof to what was originally a first-floor hall. English carpenters would make the first floor (and sometimes subsequent floors) project over the one below. This provided extra space in cities, although no one knows why it was adopted in the countryside. The Old Canonry may be the earliest surviving example of this jettying. One consequence is that the roof still does not need gutters.

A grand property indeed, and not just a home but a piece of history. But it wasn't somewhere that the Hollywood family would live indefinitely. The newspaper article formed part of a series of features – 'History For Sale' – which focussed on old houses with a history that were being sold on by their owners. After living at The Old Canonry for just a short period of time, Paul and Alexandra had decided that it was time to move on.

The feature described how they had bought the house 18 months previously in 2004 after rescuing it from a 'sad condition'. It seemed that Paul had managed to restore the property, at least in some part, to its former glory while also building some special memories there. 'This is a wonderful Christmas house,' he told the *Sunday Telegraph*. 'Our son Josh has got very attached to it; the walled garden is safe for him to play in. But with a house like this, you never own it – you are only looking after it.'

The family moved to another Grade 1-listed cottage, costing an estimated £800,000 – proving their hearts lay in Kent. And it was there that Paul would start the next phase of his career: building up a successful artisan bakery firm. It was time to capitalise on his extraordinary baking skills in a big way. Finally, he was about to run a business of his own.

# CHAPTER 6

# In the Dough

A t least for the time being, Paul's foray into the world of TV cookery seemed to have been put on the backburner. Although he had enjoyed a limited amount of success, his TV career didn't appear to have taken off in the way that he might have hoped. But there was nothing untoward about that: many cooks try to make the transition from the kitchen counter to the TV screen without half as much success even at this early stage. At least he now had an agent who would doubtless be keeping a keen eye out for future commissions. Indeed a steady trickle of TV projects would be coming his way over the next few years. While he certainly didn't make the transition to being a widely recognised TV star until *The Great British Bake Off* came into his life some years later, he would often make smaller appearances on TV shows and appear in the occasional series talking about his love of bread and baking. On top of that, he had also found a lifelong friend in James Martin.

Of course, most important of all, he and Alexandra were enjoying what seemed to be an almost perfect life in Kent and had been blessed with a baby boy. After years in Cyprus they had finally put down roots. But now Paul was looking for the next challenge.

It was then that he came upon a business idea that would, if it went to plan, see him use his innate passion and love of bakery in a way that would also net him a vast sum of money. He would start his own bakery business. Not only would Paul be his own boss for the first time in his career, but the financial rewards could also be lucrative. A successful baking firm had the potential to sell to businesses across the UK, and if that went well he could build on his reputation and even expand globally, if he so desired. Perhaps he had looked to his father for inspiration. After all, John had turned a single bakery shop in the Wirral into a profitable and much-respected business, with shops all over England. If his father could do it, so could he.

Paul was looking to produce something special. The focus would be on his one true love – bread. But it would be a special type of bread bakery: high-end 'artisan bread'. It would be a bakery that would sell all types of different bread, but the focus would be to make it a little more high-end. To the untrained eye, it might be difficult to tell the difference between sourdough and focaccia. But to an artisan bread maker – and consumer – it was these subtleties that made the products stand apart from regular, run-of-the-mill loaves.

One website describes the essence of artisan bread. 'Artisan bread is best described by thinking about the person who makes the bread,' says ArtisanBread.com. 'An artisan baker is a craftsperson who is trained to the highest ability to mix, ferment, shape and bake a hand-crafted loaf of bread. They understand the science behind the chemical reactions of the ingredients and know how to provide the best environment for the bread to develop.' Put simply, it seems the bread is baked with a little more attention to detail; with tender loving care and an understanding of the processes using the highest-quality ingredients.

The creation of artisan bread was a special process. It was a craft – something that could be learned in detail and understood as a scientific process, not just something to be done haphazardly or produced in bulk. 'A baker's work parallels that of jewellers, glass blowers or furniture makers,' the website continues. 'They all have a palette of preferred, trustworthy materials They know how to combine their materials to build something strong and at the same time delicate or elegant. Combining the raw materials in different ways will create various shapes, textures or colours. The finished product is something to be proud of when so much thought and creativity went into it.'

The dexterity required to make an artisan loaf was something a keen master baker such as Paul appreciated and understood. For him baking wasn't so much a job as a passion and a way of life.

But how can the casual eye spot the difference between artisan and everyday bread? One starting point is the ingredients used. 'There shouldn't be anything in bread besides flour, water, salt and yeast,' says ArtisanBread.com. 'If the bread is made with a sourdough there may not even be yeast in the ingredients. Flavoured breads may list other recognisable ingredients like nuts, garlic, herbs or cheese. A viennoiserie bread, for example a brioche, will include milk, butter and/or eggs. All of the ingredients should sound like familiar foods. Remember you are buying one of the oldest most basic foods there is. It wasn't necessary to add chemicals to bread for centuries and it still isn't.'

But it's not just the ingredients that determine whether or not the bread is artisan. The process by which it has been baked must also be taken into account. This includes the location where it has been baked – artisan bread cannot be mass-produced in a factory and needs tending meticulously in a small, controlled environment where individual attention is bestowed on each and every loaf, which has its own unique, irregular shape. This may sound slightly over the top, but that's the lengths an artisan baker has to go to! 'Next think about the place that the bread was made,' Artisan Bread.com continues. 'In a small artisan bakery the baker will often show you around. If the bread is made in a large factory you might not get past the front gate. An artisan bakery is small enough that it is possible to train each worker to understand the whole process of making the bread and to make small enough batches for one or two people to manage.'

And it's fair to say that for Paul the concept of artisan bread had enormous appeal. Baking was never something that he had got into to manufacture baked goods. Remember, his first experience of baking was in the family kitchen, helping his mother to make ginger biscuits. The attention to detail and the precision of each individual bake was so important to him. It's why he would later become such a meticulous judge on *The Great British Bake Off*.

And now he wanted to turn his love of baking into a business opportunity. His idea was to deliver high-quality bread to some of the biggest firms around the country. There seemed to be a growing taste for pricier, more high-end bread – something he saw as a unique opportunity to capitalise on. And so in 2007 the Artisan Bread Company was born. He set about building the business from scratch, basing it near the family home in Aylesham, Kent. Unfortunately, he soon came across a snag.

After he decided to name his business the Artisan Bread Company (which many would agree is a good name because it does exactly what it says on the tin), Paul revealed that he had to go through some legal formalities to ensure his own name, Hollywood, was on the patent. It seemed to make perfect sense – after all, his reputation was rapidly growing. However, it seemed there was a completely unforeseen setback. When Paul's lawyer tried to get the name patented, another Hollywood attempted to block it. Not another person called Hollywood, not even another business named Hollywood, but the LA neighbourhood of Hollywood in the United States of America! It was a turn of events that no one could have predicted.

Paul explained the astonishing, if somewhat hilarious, predicament he had found himself in to the *Daily Mail*.

'Hollywood stole my name,' he told the interviewer. 'When I was patenting my company about ten years ago I got a letter from lawyers for the City of West Hollywood, California. They thought I was trying to nab their business.' Surely this was a David and Goliath situation? Paul's business would be relatively tiny in comparison to the Californian Hollywood of movie studios, endless blue skies and upscale shopping. Or perhaps lawyers for the city of Hollywood had already tasted Paul's bread and were predicting great things?

Either way, he eventually won the battle. 'My patent lawyer was a very good one, and he pointed out to them that the family name has been around considerably longer than America has,' Paul told the *Daily Mail*. '"If you can prove otherwise," [the lawyer] said, "then my client will back down."' But despite winning the dispute, Paul's lawyer couldn't resist one last, playful dig. 'They surrendered,' said Paul. 'Then for fun, he sent a letter saying, "I hear you have my client's name on a mountain. Can you take that down?"'

With the dispute resolved, Paul could focus on the task at hand: baking great bread. But like all start-ups, it wasn't easy to begin with. There were tough times and he really had to put in the legwork to ensure his business was making a decent bottom line in the crucial first years. 'I have gone through some bad times with my own business,' he told the *Radio Times*. 'At one point I was working my socks off, driving, delivering, baking. It was hard, hard work. But I worked through it. Running your own bakery is hard.'

Eventually he was forced to cut costs and call on his loyal family for financial support. 'I never came close to bankruptcy but I had to cut back on staff,' he admitted. 'And when I needed equipment, I was fortunate to have family who were prepared to put their hands in their pockets. I was good at what I did and they believed in me. I stuck to it, because I didn't want to lose what I had. And I never give up.'

Gradually the business started to go from strength to strength. Paul developed the fledgling company into a well-respected brand that was making good profits and supplying big chains such as Waitrose. In an interview with the consumer trade magazine *The Grocer* in 2011, he revealed that the Artisan Bread Company was making upwards of 1,000 loaves every day. The turnover was £350,000 and he admitted that he wanted to double that figure over the coming two years. These were impressive figures – and even more impressive projections – considering how tough it had been to begin with.

But like everything in his career, it seemed when Paul put his mind to something, he always managed to master it. Naturally, his family were impressed by his success. Paul told the *Radio Times*: 'My mum is very proud of me.'

So after a tough start, it seemed the Artisan Bread Company was making excellent progress. Orders were flying in and business was booming. Paul was well and truly in the dough – literally and metaphorically!

And with the business going as well as it was, he decided that it was time to take his bread making to a whole new level. The company specialised in artisan products, but now, in 2009, Paul wished to redefine the boundaries. He came up with an idea that would set his business apart from any other artisan bakery: the recipe for what is believed to be the most expensive loaf of bread ever sold in Britain.

Costing a pricey £15 a loaf, Paul's Roquefort and almond sourdough loaf really set him apart. It cost more than ten times the price of an ordinary loaf of supermarket bread. Sourdough is widely considered one of the most expensive and, indeed, tasty of breads. The dough is fermented using naturally occurring lactobacilli and yeasts rather than the cultivated yeasts used in regular bread. As the name suggests, sourdough tends to have a mildly sour taste because of the lactic acid produced by the lactobacilli.

On top of the sourdough itself, he was careful to use only the finest ingredients. Only the best Roquefort cheese was used – purchased and imported from a producer in rural France who charged an eye-watering £15 per kilo. Meanwhile, the flour used to make the sourdough was sourced from a specialist miller in Wiltshire. No expense was spared in the creation of this loaf.

As a result of all this, Paul needed to target a group of shoppers who had that extra spending power. An expensive loaf like this needed an expensive shop. And what better place than Harrods, the upmarket store located in London's Knightsbridge? The establishment had a long-standing reputation for being the preserve of the most elite of shoppers and would be the perfect outlet.

With his keen eye for business, Paul made sure the loaf was available in time for Christmas, so as to capitalise on those shoppers who were willing to spend that little extra for the festive season. By then Britain was in the grip of the global recession, but as far as Paul was concerned, the British people still had a love of great-tasting food and he insisted that his latest creation would be a big success.

'There may be a recession, but let them eat bread,' he told the *Daily Telegraph*. 'I know it's the credit crunch and bread is obviously a staple known for being cheap. But it's a fantastic loaf – the best I've ever made. We've been conducting tastings in local delicatessens near us and the feedback is amazing – everyone loves it. And I personally don't think there's any harm in pushing the boat out and using top-quality ingredients. If you think of the ordinary loaf of bread it's quite plain and often lacking in excitement. If you were to compare it to a car it might be a Ford Fiesta, for example. But this is the Rolls-Royce of loaves.'

He also insisted that customers were getting what they paid for. Like any true artisan, he had lavished time and effort in selecting the constituents of the bread, making sure his loaf was the best money could buy.

'I have searched all over the country and Europe to make sure the ingredients are the very best available,' he explained. 'The flour I use is grade A. It has no additives, emulsifiers, E numbers or artificial flavourings. It is as close to pure as you can get.'

But it wasn't just hearsay that the bread was the most expensive you could buy in the UK – it was also officially recognised as such by the National Association of Master Bakers. President Chris Beaney commented: 'This truly is a super-specialised loaf of bread and one that has a very niche market. At £15 it certainly is an expensive option but it's all down to the ingredients. They really are a cut above. There is a growing demand for this kind of bread – it has a sourdough base which has proved very popular in recent years. Not every baker would be able to sell this kind of bread but I think most of them would certainly like to try it – it sounds very tasty indeed.'

And as far as Harrods were concerned, they were delighted that Paul had chosen their store. A spokesman said: 'At Harrods we are always on the lookout for exciting new products that are also of the best quality. This is the perfect bread for consumers wanting luxurious bread in the run-up to Christmas. At Harrods, we believe in catering for all tastes and price ranges.'

Understandably, the loaf caused a stir, and as the press clamoured to cover the story of Paul's expensive bake, the *Kentish Gazette* said: 'Crumbs! Have you seen the price of bread these days? Well take a deep breath, for this costly cob, at £15 a loaf, is not a credit crunching option. This is no ordinary bread because it is made with a special recipe created by master baker, Paul Hollywood, from Wingham, and sells in Harrods of London'. Ever the businessman, Paul told the paper: 'We are really excited about working with Harrods. They are keen to try all the new and unusual flavoured breads, like our Roquefort and almond loaf, which is presented in a red and gold box. Have a slice of it with a cup of tea and you won't want to touch your turkey.' And even if the loaf didn't fly off the shelves owing to the hefty price tag, at the very least it had generated a huge amount of publicity.

But while the Roquefort and almond loaf was certainly the most expensive loaf that Paul had ever produced, he was also coming up with other exotic recipes. Variations included a sour cherry and chocolate loaf for those with a sweet tooth, as well as rosemary and garlic bread and a special Christmas bread: apricot couronne. Shaped like a crown, he insisted that it 'could be the finest thing you taste this festive period' in the same interview with the *Kentish Times*, before adding: 'It's filled with cranberries, walnuts, almonds, apricots, macaroon and orange and lemon zest.'

It seemed Britain had embraced artisan baking. The once small industry of artisan bakeries was growing rapidly by 2011, according to a feature in *The Grocer*. 'As sales of artisan bread rise,' wrote Virginia Matthews, 'independent bakers are looking to broaden their reach to cash in on the growing appetite for tasting alternatives to the traditional white sliced loaf'.

At this point in time artisan bakers held a 5 per cent slice of the market, but were hoping to boost shares through new and innovative means. French bakery chain Paul, for example, was looking to team up with Waitrose in the hope of rolling out their products in some of the supermarket's London stores, which already stocked the artisan range from French bakery Poilâne. Another artisan bakery called Gail's was also planning to expand its chain of six stores by opening another on London's trendy Exmouth Market. However, some diehard artisan bakers believed that if they went into business with supermarkets, it would cheapen their market value. They would effectively be forced to reduce prices in order to compete with the cheaper loaves of bread typically found on supermarket shelves.

Paul waded into the discussion. 'The debate over what constitutes an authentically artisan loaf will continue forever,' he told *The Grocer*. But he insisted the issue was not whether or not artisan bakers should reduce their costs, but said it was up to supermarkets to increase the prices of more run-of-the-mill loaves. According to him, bread should be that bit more expensive as it had been sold at an 'artificially low cost' for too long.

'The price of wrapped bread was far too low for far too long and I am probably one of the only consumers in the country who applauds the fact that the cost of a factory loaf has started to rise fairly dramatically in recent months, making it on average only 20p or 30p less than one of my own standard loaves nowadays,' he told the trade journal. 'I believe it's possible for artisan bread to double its market share to 10 per cent fairly rapidly but beyond that I'd argue we need to encourage greater consumer experimentation by putting a premium on all bread.'

For his own part he was keen to stress that he didn't *always* insist on eating artisan bread – far from it. He told *The Grocer* that he preferred a Chorleywood for his own bacon sandwiches, and understood perfectly why many parents chose a white sliced loaf for their children's lunchboxes. Even so, he was keen to stress that artisan breads shouldn't 'remain the province of the well-heeled'. 'Many people living outside London and the M25 want to try something special for breakfast, and, given the reduced cost differential today, I see no reason why artisan bread shouldn't become at least a once-weekly staple for them,' he said. 'They simply need better access to something decent.'

The rise of the Artisan Bread Company from a small start-up to a big business with a high turnover proved that Paul could turn his baking skills into a lucrative enterprise. His eagerness to encourage more folk to buy artisan bread showed a strong determination to continue to develop the business.

More interestingly, he also appeared to be doing what a lot of celebrity chefs have done... but in reverse. While many TV chefs have used their newfound fame on the box to launch business opportunities, such as merchandising, product ranges and food brands, Paul was doing the opposite. Despite a brief foray into the world of TV cookery, his career path would see him launch a successful brand in the form of the Artisan Bread Company before going on to find wider fame, thanks to *The Great British Bake Off*.

In recent years other celebrity chefs such as Jamie Oliver and Nigella Lawson have become prolific in their endorsement of everything from egg timers to aprons, in addition to their books. Jamie Oliver was initially known as 'The Naked Chef' courtesy of his cockney accent, relaxed appearance and no-nonsense attitude in the kitchen, where he is happy to eschew strict weights or measurements in his recipes. Meanwhile, Nigella is the self-styled 'Domestic Goddess' whose penchant for wearing figure-hugging gowns that cling to her curves while she whips up gooey desserts attracts numerous column inches. They are each a brand, following in the footsteps of pioneer and *Bake Off* judge Mary Berry in seeing the potential to capitalise on their name.

Jamie Oliver followed a very similar template to Mary Berry in mapping out his brand with a range that includes seasonings, pasta sauces and stuffings. His books earn him millions. In 2002 Jamie set up Fifteen, a restaurant run by apprentices wishing to move away from their difficult backgrounds through what Oliver calls 'meaningful hard work'. On top of this he has become an ardent campaigner for healthy eating in schools, a passion that took him all the way to Downing Street and eventually earned him an MBE. It was a campaign that would surely not have gained so much momentum without Jamie's high profile or indeed the popularity of his trusted brand.

Another celebrity cook who has trodden a similar branding path is Nigella Lawson. Her success means her brand – Nigella – is instantly recognisable. Having written restaurant reviews for *The Spectator* and then a food column for *Vogue*, her first cookbook, *How to Eat*, sold 300,000 copies and became a bestseller. Two years later, *How to be a Domestic Goddess* won the British Book Award for Author of the Year. Literary success was accompanied by a move on screen, with a Channel 4 series called *Nigella Bites*. And then in 2002, she launched her own cookware range, Living Kitchen, which is currently valued at £7 million.

Another example of a cook developing into a brand is Delia Smith, who published her first recipe in 1969 and has since gone on to sell 14 million books. Her TV series attract millions of viewers. If any evidence was needed to prove her value as a marketing tool, her name was even included in the Collins English Dictionary in 2001, owing to the fact that it had become such a part of everyday conversation. Much has been written over the years about the so-called 'Delia Effect', in particular after the publication of her hugely successful *How To Cook* books, the first of which was released in 1998 and tied in with her TV series of the same name. The 'Delia Effect' was used to encapsulate the phenomenon where supermarket shelves were suddenly emptied of particular items featured on her shows.

There was reportedly a 10 per cent rise in egg sales in Britain off the back of the *How To Cook* series. A struggling Lancashire firm was brought back from the brink of collapse after Delia used their omelette pan on her show and described it as a 'little gem'. Sales went through the roof and the firm reported that they went from selling 200 pans a year to 90,000 in four months. Other ingredients to instantly run out of stock included cranberries – there was apparently a national shortage in 1995 – as well as vegetable bouillon powder, limes, and kitchen equipment such as pestles and mortars. Sea salt, prunes and instant mashed potato were also boosted by Delia's recommendations. The phenomenon suggested that celebrity chefs could have a powerful influence on our eating habits.

By 2001, after the third and final *How To Cook* book was published, the 'Delia Effect' had become a frequently used phrase. The BBC reported that the noun 'Delia' was included in a new edition of the Collins English Dictionary after publishers found that it had passed into everyday use. Using a computer database of 418 million words that were spoken and written in English, pooled from various television shows, books, conversations and newspapers, a staggering 700 references to 'Delia' were found. Other entries centred around

Delia's name included a 'Delia dish', described as a recipe or in the 'style of cooking of British cookery writer Delia Smith', as well as 'Delia power' and 'Doing a Delia'.

Christmas sales have been transformed by the power of Jamie, Nigella and Delia. Both Jamie and Nigella recommend goose fat to crispen up roast potatoes, and, as a result, supermarkets have recorded unprecedented sales around this time of year. The *Daily Telegraph* reported that, at Sainsbury's, sales of cinnamon sticks were up 200 per cent on the same period the previous year, while sales of Marsala wine, an ingredient in Delia's panettone trifle, went through the roof by 300 per cent. Sales of pickled walnuts doubled after Delia coupled it with braised venison in 1994. The newspaper reported that her recipe for chestnut cupcakes also caused shoppers to stock up on new ingredients, including crème de marrons, a sweetened chestnut purée, and chestnut flour, which hadn't been widely stocked until Delia's successful TV series, *Classic Christmas*. A spokesperson for the supermarket chain told the *Daily Telegraph*: 'Every year we get calls about the ingredients that feature in celebrity chef tips. In the past we have answered calls on goose fat, cranberries and, last year, semolina due to Nigella Lawson's roast potato tip, with sales shooting through the roof. This year calls have led to us stocking the unusual chestnut flour in our special selection range.'

Paul had, of course, intended to make the most of the Christmas market with his various exotic breads. He too knew how to turn food into a moneyspinner. By 2010, the Artisan Bread Company was going from strength to strength. It seemed he no longer needed TV stardom to make a living: his business was already doing that for him.

It was somewhat ironic then that just around the corner an opportunity to become a true TV star would present itself. Brand Hollywood was about to get an unexpected, though enormously welcome, boost.

# CHAPTER 7

# The *Bake Off* Takes Off

With the Artisan Bread Company making good profits and also managing to hit headlines thanks to his creative ideas, and his family life also in tip top shape, Paul couldn't be happier. On top of this, he was able to do a little bit of TV here and there. Slowly but surely he was becoming a well-known face, particularly when it came to baking.

Although he didn't realise it at the time, in 2010 he was on the brink of becoming a huge household name. While he had tried with limited success to become a fully fledged TV personality, an amazing opportunity was about to present itself. It would see him become, once and for all, a staple on British TV. A new series called *The Great British Bake Off* was being developed and Paul was destined to be an integral part of it. In fact, the show would propel him to a level of stardom that, quite frankly, he would never have imagined possible.

It all started in the summer of 2010 in the offices of an independent British TV company called Love Productions. The firm was developing a great reputation throughout the UK television industry. Founded in 2005, it had quickly cemented its place as one of the premier production companies in Britain. It had built up a reputation for gritty reality TV documentaries, which had been making waves with viewers and critics alike. Among them was *Underage and Having Sex*, which took its starting point from the statistic that one in three British youngsters will have sex before their sixteenth birthday. Then there was *8 Boys And Wanting A Girl*, which visited the home of 43-year-old Wendy Bowen. As the title suggests, she had given birth to eight sons but was desperate to conceive a daughter. In fact, according to the programme synopsis, her ticking biological clock meant her quest had 'turned into an obsession'.

There was something about Love Productions that set it apart from the crowd. It wasn't afraid to get to grips with controversial real-life issues nor did it seem at all concerned if that meant not being considered particularly 'worthy' in terms of output by some critics. Ratings were what mattered in the TV industry and Love Productions' shows were getting these in spades. Now, in the summer of 2010, they were looking for something different. The creative directors behind the company's success needed a huge new hit – and they thought they might just have the answer.

The genre of show they decided to focus on was one that

had become hugely popular over the last two decades. By then it was impossible to turn on the TV at almost any time of day in the UK without stumbling across some sort of cookery show, be it one where the viewers were given recipes to follow in their own kitchens or a more competitive, reality-style set-up where contestants vied to be the very best and beat the rivals.

A decision was made by the powers that be at Love Productions that the time was right to move in this direction. They wanted a competitive cookery show but one with a twist. A resurgent love of all things retro in Britain meant that baking was back in fashion. What's more, the biting recession would soon encourage people to stay at home and have fun for free. Combining these two elements – competitive cookery and baking – seemed the perfect recipe for success. And so *The Great British Bake Off* was born. The title was similar to *The Great British Menu*, another TV cookery competition that saw top British chefs compete for the chance to cook one course of a four-course banquet for a range of people, including HM The Queen and the British Ambassador to France. Talk about pressure!

Announcing the show in mid-2010, Love Productions' managing director Richard McKerrow promised a 'warm and celebratory' series that would 'tell the history of Britain through baking'. He added: 'Baking is quintessentially British and it's the perfect feel-good subject for these rather straitened times. We want nothing less than to get the whole country baking again.'

And it didn't take long for the show to be commissioned by

a major TV channel. BBC2 immediately snapped it up. It came as no surprise that the broadcaster would go for *The Great British Bake Off* as it had long been the natural home of major cookery competition shows – especially wholesome ones like this. The channel had been the birthplace of *MasterChef* in 1990, which had recently returned to screens and proved a big success.

With the show commissioned, it was time for the producers to decide on the judges. As with all reality shows, success would stand or fall on who was on the judging panel. So who would be their answer to Simon Cowell? After taking some time to consider this, the producers decided Paul Hollywood was the right man for the job. Not only did he have a down-to-earth, straight-talking personality, but also an intimate knowledge of baking that meant that he would know the bakes expected of the contestants inside out. The perfect fit, he ticked all the boxes.

British comedian and broadcaster Sue Perkins, who would later be picked to co-present the show, played a major role in Paul's TV breakthrough. Previously, she had met him on a number of occasions, having been involved in a string of food programmes. Already in talks with the producers about her own role, she suggested him as a good choice of judge. Perhaps it was Paul's single-minded passion for his craft that had sealed the deal. In one interview with the *Daily Mail* he had said: 'All I want to do is bake. Whether I do that on TV or on the moon, I'm still just a baker.' His straight-talking manner would no doubt balance fellow judge Mary Berry's poise, politeness and gentle nature.

Paul explained in an interview with the *Kent Messenger* how it all came about. 'I was approached by one of the presenters, Sue Perkins, to take part, as she had seen some of my stuff on the Good Food Channel. The BBC then rang me to talk me through the idea and introduce me to fellow judge, baking writer Mary Berry. Then, at the start of April, we began filming around the country for the six-part series.'

It was a done deal. Paul had secured his big break at last, and he would be partnered by another great, well-known lover of all things baked: Mary Berry. It was vital, as far as the producers were concerned, that he was alongside someone who was established and well known in the baking world. And Mary was already well established in the British consciousness owing to her incredible, illustrious career as the doyenne of baking. Revered for her straightforward recipes by enthusiasts up and down the country, she had sold over 5 million books around the world. Her 50-plus titles, including her first book, the *Hamlyn All Colour Cookbook*, had been translated into a string of foreign languages.

In addition she was a staple on British cookery and lifestyle shows, often whipping up recipes for audiences on programmes such as ITV's *The Alan Titchmarsh Show* and the massively popular *This Morning*. She had also hosted her own series across various networks. Another reason for Mary's rise to becoming a household name was her love of the AGA. Over the years she had become a passionate proponent of the trusty heat storage stove and cooker, running workshops for would-be bakers at her home just outside of London and penning numerous books on the subject too. Then there was her personal life. In addition to her vast array of experience in the kitchen, Mary had also had her fair share of ups and downs in life. Tragically she had lost her 19-year-old son William when he died in a car accident while home for the holidays from his studies in Bristol. Mary had life experience – something that made her a real person and someone with whom the public, who had adored her for years, could empathise. In short, she seemed like the perfect fit to judge alongside Paul.

Paul and Mary each had their own strengths; they were similar but different. And they worked a treat together during the various screen tests the producers put them through and the audition process for the show's contestants, showing a natural chemistry right from the start. As far as everyone was concerned, this was a match made in heaven.

With the judging panel in place, all the producers now needed before they launched was a presenter or, indeed, presenters. Sue Perkins' name was in the frame. Born in 1969 in Croydon, south London, she was educated at the independent school Croham Hurst For Girls, later winning a place to read English at New Hall, at the University of Cambridge, graduating in 1990. It was while at university that she really developed her love of entertaining – and discovered she had a knack for it. She was a member of Cambridge Footlights, the amateur dramatics club with a prestigious reputation responsible for launching the careers of stars such as John Cleese, Stephen Fry, Hugh Laurie, Emma Thompson and *Downton*-turned-Hollywood heart-throb Dan Stevens, to name but a few. All had belonged to Footlights while at Cambridge and had gone on to achieve remarkable success.

It was while she was a member of Footlights that Sue, who later went on to become president, met fellow student and actress Mel Giedroyc. Born in 1968 in Epsom, Surrey, Mel's father was a history writer of Polish-Lithuanian descent who came to England in 1947. Growing up, Mel had shown a real flair for learning and speaking foreign languages. After studying at Oxford High School for Girls, she won a place at Cambridge to read Italian language and literature at New Hall.

Performing together for Footlights, the pair soon established not just a solid friendship but a promising comedy partnership too. After graduating they decided to become an official duo, and set about pursuing joint success. The endless gigging at stand-up comedy events eventually paid off when they were picked to pen material for the BBC television series *French and Saunders*. The famous sketch show starred another all-female comedy duo, Dawn French and Jennifer Saunders, who had achieved enormous popularity and success. As Mel and Sue continued to flourish, they would find themselves compared to their comedy heroines.

In fact, things really started to take off when they secured their very own TV show. And as with both Mary and Paul, it would be on daytime TV. In 1997 they launched the popular lunchtime show *Light Lunch*, on Channel 4. It was an extremely simple concept, but one that really worked. Celebrity chefs would cook lunch for the duo's celebrity guests, bringing together food and chat. Unlike Mary and Paul, Mel and Sue did none of the cooking, though. Their irreverent, humorous style proved an unlikely hit with daytime audiences. Later, the show was moved to an early evening slot and renamed *Late Lunch*. To add to the banter, studio audiences were also expected to bring in their own lunch to eat during the show, and were each given £3 to cover the cost of this. They were encouraged to bring in unusual food, their own creations, or food in some way relating to that day's celebrity guest. The most creative ideas would be shown on camera.

After a successful two-year run, Mel and Sue were very much on the radar of top TV executives, who were clamouring to sign them up for future projects. In 1999, Channel 4's rival network ITV won the battle, getting them on board to front a new comedy panel show called *Casting Couch*. The girls hosted the show while radio DJ Chris Moyles and former socialite Tamara Beckwith were the captains of the show's two teams. The main topic of discussion was celebrity gossip and each team has to vie against the other to prove they know more about the world of showbiz.

It was a great opportunity for the girls to reach a wider, more adult audience, as the programme aired in a late evening slot. Unfortunately, though, for some it didn't quite live up to the hype. The ratings did not meet expectations and ITV bosses chose not to commission it again after the first series. Despite this setback, Mel and Sue carried on unfazed. Other side projects included returning to where it all started, appearing together again in a French and Saunders *Mamma Mia!* sketch for Comic Relief in March 2009, and on various radio programmes. The double act proved particularly popular with Radio 4 listeners.

Their friendship remained as solid and steadfast as ever, but before too long, Mel and Sue decided they wanted to take on solo projects. While Sue has tried her hand at a series of different things, including a stint on *Celebrity Big Brother* and presenting on the now-defunct Channel 4 breakfast show *RI:SE*, she quickly found a niche presenting food shows. In April 2007, she took part in *Edwardian Supersize Me* for the BBC with food critic Giles Coren. The unusual programme involved the pair eating the equivalent of a wealthy Edwardian couple's diet, while dressed in traditional clothes from the era. It proved a winning formula, and the following year she and Giles returned with a new series called *The Supersizers Go...* In this, they would spend a week eating food based upon certain diets. The first programme saw them survive for a week on Second World War rations. In the second episode, they moved back in time to the English Restoration period, followed by the Victorian ages, the 1970s, the Elizabethan and Regency periods. Then, in 2006, Sue once again displayed her love for all things culinary by appearing on *Celebrity MasterChef*.

Meanwhile, Mel worked on a range of programmes including co-presenting a daytime chat show and being cast in a BBC sitcom. She also starred in three series of the twice BAFTA-nominated cult sketch show *Sorry I've Got No Head*, as well as the West End musical *Eurobeat* and popular teen drama, *Sadie J*.

But after working separately for some four years, it looked like a reunion could be on the cards. With Sue already in talks with the producers behind *The Great British Bake Off*, it was decided she would be paired with a co-host. Keen to make sure that a show about baking didn't become too serious or staid, they wanted presenters they could rely on to keep it light and good-humoured. In the end it was an obvious decision – Mel and Sue were a winning combination. Sue first hinted about their reunion when she appeared on *Friday Night with Jonathan Ross*, saying they would be working on something together in 2010. While excited at the prospect of working with Mel again, she did admit in an interview with TV industry magazine *Broadcast* that she also found it daunting because of the time that had passed. She admitted: 'We'd both changed hugely as individuals.' Speaking ahead of the first series, Sue added that she wasn't sure whether they would work together full time, but they were excited about *The Great British Bake Off*. 'We're keen to keep our new identities but the door's definitely open,' she insisted.

With all the judges and presenters in place, the producers could set about creating a format for the show. But there was one important element they were still missing: contestants. They were looking for would-be master bakers who were keen to show their flair, originality and creativity over a series of weeks in the hope of being crowned the winner. And there was no shortage to choose from. More than 1,000 hopefuls put their names forward for the audition process before being whittled down to 10 lucky finalists. Getting to that stage was no mean feat. In this particular reality TV show, there was no room for novelty contestants or sob stories. Anna Beattie, the executive producer and creator of *The Great British Bake Off* concept, told the *Daily Telegraph*: 'Every person who makes it into the marquee has passed a rigorous series of tests.'

And Anna – who came up with the idea for the show after talking to a friend who had seen 'bake offs' in America, where they were hugely popular – wasn't exaggerating. The contestants all had to fill out a long application form, which, if it met the requirements, allowed them through to the next stage. They would then be quizzed by one of the show's researchers in a 45-minute telephone interview. Only then would potential contestants be invited to London with two of their most successful 'bakes' to see if their culinary skills really were up to scratch. Following this there was a screen test and a further interview with a senior producer.

Even after all this, there was more. If the would-be baking superstars ticked all of these boxes, they then had to go through to a second audition – the most nerve-wracking of all. This involved baking two recipes for none other than Mary Berry and Paul Hollywood, this time in front of rolling cameras, to see how they would interact with the two judges and how they would come across on screen. And the final hurdle, which all contestants have to pass, is a forensic interview with one of the show's psychologists. The producers have a duty of care to all contestants and they wanted to make sure they could cope with the stresses, strains and overall pressure of being filmed for up to 16 hours a day, potentially for weeks on end. No wonder contestants on reality shows are often told they're 'all winners' for even getting on the show in the first place!

Finally, after the lengthy audition process, Mary and Paul had their 10 contestants. They comprised Welsh bus driver Mark Withers, Scottish freelance food writer Lea Harris,

Marks & Spencer commercial manager Miranda Gore Browne, Solihull housewife Jasminder Randhawa, David Chambers from Milton Keynes, Annetha Mills, Manchester police sergeant Louise Brimelow, shop owner Jonathan Shepherd, fourth-generation baker Ruth Clemens and debt collector Edd Kimber. Over the course of six episodes they would get to battle it out, with Mary and Paul eventually finding a winner.

Before too long, filming swung into action. In the first series, the show visited a different location around the UK each week. First up was the Cotswolds. Other locations included Sandwich and Sarre Mill in Thanet, Kent, with a view to enabling the contestants to find out about a place where traditional baking skills are still used. They would later cook puddings in Bakewell, pasties in Cornwall and scones at Scone Palace, in Perthshire, Scotland. The travelling alone must have proved exhausting, but with filming under way, there was no time to think about this for the set was a hive of activity and there was baking to be done.

Mel and Sue kept the atmosphere jovial and lively with their witty asides and comic interludes, whether the cameras were rolling or switched off. In particular, they became adept at teasing Paul, gently poking fun at his hairstyle and patting him affectionately as they prepared to film their own segments. Meanwhile, food producers were constantly on hand to help. While the contestants are by and large left to their own devices, the food producers aid anyone who finds themselves in trouble, giving tips on how to save a recipe or providing new ingredients. 'We help the bakers to a certain degree,'

Faenia Moore, the programme's home economist, told the *Daily Telegraph* in an interview. 'We do show the disasters, but you don't want to set anyone up for a fall.'

The first contestants to leave the show were Matt and Lea, both evicted at the end of the opening episode. After her exit, Lea told *The Scotsman*: 'Let's just say cakes are very temperamental and every one of the cakes looked completely different from the other. It was quite stressful and there were some tears, but when you're on camera and cooking to a time limit it is quite stressful. It's just off camera, but I managed to drop my signature bake – pistachio and cranberry cake – on the floor. And I almost set my clothes on fire, which you can't see on TV. With five minutes to spare, I managed to stick the five bits of my cake back together.'

Unfortunately for Lea and her fellow contestants, Paul had little time for excuses. He soon developed a reputation for being quite strict, but insisted he simply wanted to provide constructive criticism so they could learn and improve. Defending his approach, he said: 'It's not personal, it's just about what they do. Some programmes have a pop at the person themselves but I give an honest opinion and maybe they've never had an honest opinion before. That's part of it and, if they get upset, it's a good thing. If they didn't get upset I'd be more worried. If they did nothing they're never going to get better.' In contrast to other reality shows, *The Great British Bake Off* took no pleasure in humiliating its contestants. Paul was simply being honest and proved himself a natural-born judge. In an interview with the *Sunday Mirror* he added: 'I judge the bake and not the person. It is all about what's on the plate. I am more than happy to judge. I'll judge anything. Even this morning, when a croissant was put on my plate, I was judging it before I even picked it up. I am judgmental – it comes with the territory.'

Mary Berry provided the perfect balance, and although the pair more often than not agreed, they would occasionally find themselves at odds because of their different baking backgrounds. Paul explained: 'Mary came from a home cooking background and I came from a professional baking background – I won't make one cake, I'll make 50. So I'll look at it from a business point of view.'

But one thing they didn't disagree on was the lunch menu. With his new job involving tasting dozens and dozens of bakes each day, Paul was keen to keep an eye on his weight and so he followed Mary's lead, who stays trim with regular tennis sessions and sensibly sized portions. He said: 'Having a good understanding of what I'm eating makes a huge difference. When we're filming I only have a small taste of each bake and for lunch I try to have the same thing that Mary's eating – healthy meals, like salads.'

His touching camaraderie with his co-presenter and passion for the job in hand meant that Paul appeared to be thoroughly enjoying the process of working on *The Great British Bake Off*. Speaking to the *Daily Mail*, he described the atmosphere on set as 'lovely and completely genuine', adding that Mel and Sue are like his 'naughty sisters'. He went on to say: 'They're always pulling faces, or winding me up, and I have to say, "Hey, you two, shush!" We have some real giggles. What you see on screen is genuine. A couple of times I've rolled out of that tent in tears from laughing so much.'

After months of filming, the series was scheduled to have its transmission date – 17 August 2010. Despite all the hype and preparation no one knew for sure whether *The Great British Bake Off* would be a success, but thankfully for all those involved it went on to become a huge hit – both in the ratings and with the critics. The first episode gained a very respectable 2.24 million viewers, but off the back of rave reviews, these figures shot up to an even more impressive 3 million in the second episode, which was sustained for the rest of the series. Naturally, both the controllers at BBC2 and the producers behind the show couldn't have been more delighted.

Critics are often harder to impress than viewers, but in this case, the reviews were also overwhelmingly positive. In particular, they focussed on Paul's brilliant relationship with Mary. Despite their ups and downs, their easy rapport translated well to the screen and made them a formidable duo. The *Guardian* described their double act as the 'secret weapon' of the show, going so far as to say that it was potentially one of the best judging combinations to have appeared on a reality TV show. And others agreed. The *Leicester Mercury* declared: 'Think *MasterChef* but with bread and cakes. With the competition being judged by Mary Berry, the undisputed Queen of Cakes, and Paul Hollywood, one of Britain's leading artisan bakers, the ten contestants have a lot to prove as they push their baking skills to the limit.'

The show prompted debate about the relative merits of

different approaches to baking. Later in the series, Anne Harrison from the Women's Institute said in the *Guardian*: 'The judges on *The Great British Bake Off* have very different styles. Mary Berry is someone even I would be nervous to cook for. The other judge, Paul Hollywood, has obviously spent his life in commercial baking. I don't always agree with him. To test a scone, the WI teaches that you don't need to cut it with a knife – you should be able to pull it apart along its natural split. Hollywood said that was wrong – but if you cut a scone with a knife, it compacts the texture as you press down. It's the same with gingerbread.'

Eventually Edd Kimber, a 26-year-old debt collector who worked for a Yorkshire bank, was victorious. An unlikely star baker you might think, but he excelled at every stage of the competition. His bakes, Mary and Paul agreed, were the standout stars; neither could fault him. But Edd was doubly delighted with his win for it meant that he could give up his day job, something he loathed. 'It was the worst job ever – I absolutely hated it,' he told the *Daily Telegraph* some months after he won series one. 'People would swear at me hourly and they'd send you round to people's houses in pairs in case things turned nasty. I used to spend most of my time looking up recipes online – I'm surprised they didn't fire me.'

Perhaps the real power of *The Great British Bake Off* was proven when, within 12 months of his victory, Edd had given up being a debt collector and instead had a recipe book in the shops, entitled *The Boy Who Bakes*. He was also running a series of cookery classes and appearing at food roadshows up and down the length of Britain. Keen to capitalise on his success, he launched his own brand for his produce too, simply called 'The Boy Who Bakes'. Explaining the thought process behind the name, he told the *Daily Telegraph* with a laugh: 'Well, I am a boy and I do bake. I wanted to make it clear that anyone can bake. In the past it's been associated with housewives and the Women's Institute but these days you get bakers from all walks of life.'

And that, it seemed, was the beauty of *The Great British Bake Off*. Finally, baking was no longer reserved for housewives in the kitchen: it was cool, trendy, something that even young men could enjoy. After ticking all the boxes – ratings, great reviews and cultural impact – it was no surprise that BBC2 were quick to snap up a second series of *Bake Off* for 2011.

# CHAPTER 8

# The *Bake Off* Continues

It seemed that viewers couldn't get enough of *The Great British Bake Off*, and in particular Paul and Mary's on-screen chemistry. It was obvious the show would be recommissioned and make a triumphant return to the TV screens the following year. For the makers behind it, this was a total no-brainer. But it seemed that viewers wouldn't have to wait as long as a year in order to see Paul and Mary back on their screens.

The demand was so high, BBC2 commissioned a one-off documentary called *The Great British Wedding Cake*. It aired on 20 April 2011 and saw Paul reunited with Mary as they explored the history of wedding cakes around the country. They charted the wedding cake's history, from its earliest incarnation as the Tudor bride cake that weighed a ton and was baked wrapped in pastry. And they revealed the story that is said to have caused the creation of the classic tiered wedding cake – a baker who spied a London church from his window and fashioned his wedding cake in its image. On top of that they regaled audiences with tales of how Queen Victoria introduced the world to royal icing. And they also revealed how the rise in popularity of second marriages led to the huge range of wedding cakes available today. Keen to extend the success of their previous series, the charismatic duo reunited with the three finalists from *Bake Off* to set them a one-off challenge to bake a wedding cake. The ratings were moderate at 1.6 million but served to build the excitement for the second series of *The Great British Bake Off*, which was just around the corner. And while the first outing had been an unrivalled success, the show was about to get even bigger.

Keen to capitalise on the first series, the producers wanted to make the second show bigger and better than before. The first change they made was the number of contestants. It was decided that the number of people competing would be upped from 10 to 12. The long audition process kicked off and finally an eclectic group of would-be master bakers was selected after much deliberation. They included Janet Basu, Yasmin Limbert, Mary-Anne Boermans, Holly Bell, Joanne Wheatley, Keith Batsford, Simon Blackwell, Robert Billington, Jason White, Urvashi Roe, Ben Frazer and Ian Vallance.

For his part, while Paul was delighted with the success of the show, he was also baffled that such a simple format could become so big. Speaking to the *Sun*, he explained that it was a 'unique thing that makes it a success – it's a mixture of all the different elements. The music, the setting, the tent, the challenges, the contestants, the presenters [Mel Giedroyc and Sue Perkins] and the judges – it's the whole thing together. If you took out one of the cogs, it wouldn't work.'

But it obviously *was* working – so much so that for the second outing the producers decided it was time to increase the number of episodes too. This time the series would consist of 10 episodes, rather than six. The extra four episodes were in response to the public's demand for the show. Of course the first series had been an unknown quantity – when the BBC had commissioned it, they had high hopes for the show although they didn't know how it would fare with viewers. But after overwhelming support from fans and critics alike, it seemed like a natural thing to order in more episodes.

The final ingredient in the pre-production process that the producers had to work out was where they were going to film the second series. But having spent the first series visiting the country's baking hot spots, the format needed freshening up. Constantly moving filming around the country was fine if there were only six episodes, but it might become tiring and expensive when there were an extra four to film.

So it was decided that rather than turn *The Great British Bake Off* into a roadshow, the whole series would be filmed in one location. After toying with various possible settings, the producers decided on Valentines Mansion, a seventeenth-century mansion house in Valentines Park, in Redbridge, Greater London. The Grade II listed building was built in 1696 for Lady Tillotson, widow of the Archbishop of Canterbury, but centuries later underwent extensive refurbishment financed by the Heritage Lottery Fund and the London Borough of Redbridge. Steeped in rich history, the beautiful house would provide a quintessentially British backdrop for the *Bake Off*, and it was here that the TV crews behind the show prepared for what would prove to be another hugely successful series before filming got under way in the early summer of 2011.

And as series two started to air in August that year, it seemed to be even more popular than the first series. Viewing figures soared. The first episode got more than 3.1 million, rising steadily to a peak of just over 5 million in episode eight. It was better than anyone could have hoped for.

Understandably, as other networks and channels started to see Paul's popularity soar – and the effect his presence was having on *The Great British Bake Off*'s ratings – they began to make a play for him to see if they could persuade him to join their channel. The *Daily Mirror* reported that in particular Channel 4 were very keen to sign him up and poach him away from the Beeb. Specifically, the report in the red-top newspaper claimed that Jay Hunt, the boss at Channel 4, had offered Paul a lucrative contract that according to the paper was worth a reported £500,000. Apparently, according to the newspaper, Hunt – who had previously been Controller of the BBC – had a reputation for luring BBC talent away from the Corporation and to Channel 4. Specifically he had managed to win over the likes of the consumer champion Mary Portas and businesswoman Hilary Devey. The critics had apparently dubbed Channel 4 'BBC Lite'. Of course it was an eye-watering sum and one that no one – least of all Paul – could ever have imagined he would have been earning when he first started out jamming donuts for his dad in the Wirral.

But Paul being Paul, he remained loyal to *The Great British Bake Off* and the BBC. The report in the *Daily Mirror* said: '*Great British Bake Off*'s Paul Hollywood has landed extra dough to stay with the BBC after Channel 4 tried to poach him.' It went on to say that, despite the big money offer from the rival channel, Paul had settled for a salary increase from his current employer, turning down the opportunity to move channels. Now, the report said, he had settled for a package worth £300,000 with the BBC. The newspaper quoted a BBC insider who said: 'It's fantastic Paul is staying with the BBC.'

So the deal was done and Paul would remain with the Beeb. And as his popularity continued to grow with the ratings, on screen the drama surrounding *The Great British Bake Off* reached its climax and the excitement was at fever pitch. As more and more people tuned in to witness what culinary delights would be whipped up week after week, the competition was getting intense. After Janet Basu unexpectedly crashed out of the competition, three women remained – Jo Wheatley, Mary-Anne Boermans and Holly Bell. They were all popular with viewers and critics alike.

Writing in the *Mail on Sunday*, Tom Parker Bowles noted this, as well as the way in which baking had brought out a drama that simply could not be scripted: 'There's Joanne, the pretty housewife who longs for a career. And Holly, precise and methodical, a perfectionist to the very marrow. And Mary-Anne, a culinary bibliophile who veers towards the experimental. All are modest and, in a thoroughly self-effacing way, desperate to win. TV chefs may shout, curse and hurl pans. TV bakers, on this evidence, are the epitome of good manners. Maternal is very much the new macho. But that is not to say that the contestants aren't, at times, overwhelmed by their emotions. There may not be tantrums, but there were plenty of tears as the weeks wore on.'

Parker Bowles went on to explain that baking itself is temperamental and a matter of science rather than art. While exact measurements are unnecessary for a stew, if you put the wrong amount of yeast in bread, disaster follows. He added: 'I have always been rather afraid of baking. I may be utterly confident about throwing together a pasta sauce, grilling a fish or roasting a joint, but ask me to make puff pastry and I will run for the hills. But, right now, baking is very much back in vogue.'

But while all three contestants were likeable, it was Essex-born Jo who would triumph when the final was screened on 13 October. Aged 41 at the time of filming, she was affectionately described as the 'youngest grandmother in the competition'. 'My nan has always been my inspiration for baking,' said Jo in an interview with the *Brentwood Gazette*. 'She would always make pastry and is a really good baker. I would go over to hers most weekends – she would make tarts and give me the off-cuts of the pastry to make jam tarts. I've always baked, ever since then.'

Jo had married her husband Richard at the age of 17 and settled down before having three boys: Billy, Jesse and Dylan. Rather than pursue a career, she had dedicated her life to being a full-time housewife. It was her typically down-to-earth manner that made her such a hit with viewers. One example of her likeable personality was in an interview with the *Mail On Sunday*, where Jo explained how her kids come home from school and give her marks out of ten for the meals she cooks for them. She said: 'It makes me feel like putting their heads in the dinner.' She had also experienced some tough times. Her husband had got involved in crime and was sentenced to seven years' imprisonment for his part in a money-laundering racket – something the tabloid press would later seize on after Jo became popular on the *Bake Off*. In typically dignified style, she kept going and after 25 years of dedicating her life to her family, her sons and friends had encouraged her to apply for the show.

'I just entered on a whim, I didn't think too much about it. I Googled it and got the application form,' she told the *Brentwood Gazette*. 'I did wonder about entering or not, but I clicked the "yes" button in the end.'

The show's producers had loved her backstory, and, despite her initial nervousness, she went down a storm with Paul and Mary at the final auditions. She was selected for the competition and now it was her time to shine.

Described in the press as 'sweet-faced and preternaturally girly', Jo's bakes were almost always near perfect throughout the course of the series. That's not to say she didn't make mistakes and at times even seemed to come close to letting the pressure of the show get to her. This was particularly apparent on one occasion. During week six of the competition, and moments before Paul and Mary were due to start the judging process, Jo hit disaster. She had made an ambitious tower of cream-stuffed profiteroles as well as a limoncello and white chocolate croquembouche – a stunning cone-shaped tower of choux-pastry balls often served at weddings in Italy and France. But suddenly, seemingly out of nowhere, her creation had collapsed and couldn't be salvaged. After the slight disaster, she was still saved by Paul and Mary, and Jo decided it was time to relax a bit more.

'It was funny, in the final I baked like I do at home,' she told the *Brentwood Gazette*. 'I think I felt by then I'd done the whole thing and experienced every bit of it. So on the final day, I didn't put the pressure on myself, I just enjoyed it. I didn't mind whether I came first, second or third, I really was just happy to have got that far. I didn't think I'd won. I heard them call out my name but I thought maybe they were doing it in reverse order. I looked up and saw my kids jumping up and down and my friends all cheering, and then I realised. It was an amazing feeling.'

As far as Paul was concerned, Jo was the natural winner too. After she was crowned, he didn't hold back in his praise for her. He said: 'Her progression in the whole *Bake Off* has been superb. Technical ability, and the precision, and the flavour, all thrown in... superb.' Mary added: 'She has achieved great heights, I hope she's chuffed to bits.' Speaking at the end of the show, an emotional Jo said: 'I feel really, really emotional, I just feel totally overwhelmed. Total delight. I feel really proud of myself.' And with her newfound confidence came new opportunities for Jo. To begin with, she set up a blog called Jo's Blue AGA, dedicated to giving advice, tips and recipes to other heat storage cooker lovers. Off the back of it, she secured the chance to hold a series of workshops in cupcake decorating, as well as Christmas hamper baking. Classes soon became fully booked as they were snapped up. But this was just the beginning of Jo's blossoming career as a celebrity baker.

Seeing how popular she was becoming, a publishing house approached Jo to write her own book. She jumped at the chance and, in 2012, she released *A Passion For Baking*, initially exclusively through supermarket Sainsbury's before becoming available in all good bookshops. During its first week of release the book flew up *The Sunday Times* Bestseller List to number two in the non-fiction charts. Suddenly she was giving Paul and Mary a run for their money. 'I never dreamt I'd be able to write a book,' she told the *Brentwood Gazette*. 'It's easy to follow, with not too many ingredients and some really good flavours. That's how I wanted the book to be, very down-to-earth and practical. It covers all aspects of baking. I thought about what I would want to do if I did a cookery book and this is it.'

The aim of the book was to appeal to as broad a cross section of bakers as possible. Jo wanted it to cater for complete novices who had never been near an oven all the way up to experienced bakers. 'The recipes are achievable for everyone. The response to the book and my blog has been amazing. On Twitter and Facebook, the reactions have been fantastic. I can't describe how wonderful it's been. I pinch myself every day that I'm getting to do this. But the more you get to write about something you like doing, the more you find out and the more doors and avenues open up for you. I pushed myself to come up with different ideas and recipes and really enjoyed doing it. It's given me a whole new purpose; I can experiment and have a reason to now.'

Jo now teaches baking masterclasses from her home in Essex and they quickly became a huge hit with the public, often booked up weeks and months in advance.

The popularity of *The Great British Bake Off* had transformed Jo from a stay-at-home mum to a household name with a successful writing and teaching career. There was no better example of how a popular TV show could make such a big difference to an individual's life. The actual prize might not have been anything substantial, but the rewards afterwards were huge. After the end of series two, TV critic Kevin O'Sullivan noted in his *Sunday Mirror* column: 'More than 5 million cake fans tuned in to *The Great British Bake Off* to see Essex mum Jo win TV's worst-ever trophy. Wooden spoons inside a see-through sphere with some sort of lemon squeezer shoved on the top. Eight weeks of hard kitchen graft and this is all she gets! But I guess that's the charm of this innocent slice of Middle England. No big-money prizes, no claptrap about changing lives, no idiot minor celebs spewing meaningless clichés. Just a good old-fashioned village-hall cooking contest. Set your ovens to 2012. This is one programme cash-strapped BBC2 won't be axing.'

It was an astute comment because the show would keep on growing. Another series was commissioned for 2012. But before then, like all popular reality shows, there would be a couple of spin offs in the form of the *Junior Bake Off* and *The Great Sport Relief Bake Off*. The first of these kicked off soon after the second series of *Great British Bake Off* had come to an end. Mary and Paul returned to judge a group of young bakers as they went through the same process as the adults had done on the actual show. For the youngsters the demands were less daunting, however. Rather than elaborate tower cakes and pastries with expensive ingredients, the kids were set challenges of baking far simpler dishes. But the idea behind the show remained the same and it was screened on the children's TV channel CBBC.

Then, in January 2012, celebrities competed on *The Great Sport Relief Bake Off*, to tie in with Sport Relief, the BBC's annual charity fundraising event. The celebrity would-be bakers included TV journalist Anita Rani, actresses Angela Griffin and Sarah Hadland, former *Strictly Come Dancing* judge and choreographer Arlene Phillips, botanist James Wong, garden designer Joe Swift, BBC journalist Fi Glover, *Apprentice* finalist Saira Khan, curator Gus Casely-Hayford, fashion designer and writer Pearl Lowe and weatherman Alex Deakin. Anita Rani eventually won the four-episode miniseries. Speaking about the celebrity special, Paul said that the rules were not so tough for the celebrities because, after all, it was a charity event. Nevertheless, he did maintain his usual meticulous standards. 'We relaxed the rules a little as it's a Comic Relief special, but Mary and I still judge all the bakes properly,' Paul told the *Sun* newspaper. 'I know people sometimes call me "Mr Nasty", but I feel it's important to be honest when judging – both the bakers and the viewers will learn from mistakes.'

Once the Comic Relief episode was behind the production

team, all eyes were on the next proper series of the show. And by the summer of 2011, preparations were once again in full swing for the return of *The Great British Bake Off*. Like the second series, there were 12 contestants who competed across 10 episodes. This time the filming moved out into the countryside to Harptree Court in picturesque East Harptree, Somerset. Originally built in 1798, Harptree Court was an award-winning country house that, ordinarily, functioned as a luxury bed and breakfast retreat. This time the contestants coming under Mary and Paul's watchful gaze were Natasha Stringer, Cathryn Dresser, Peter Maloney, Victoria Chester, Stuart Marston-Smith, Manisha Parmar, Sarah-Jane Willis, Ryan Chong, Danielle Bryden, Brendan Lynch, James Morton and John Whaite. The series hit screens in August – and by now it had become a staple of British TV.

But while the ratings were better than ever, and fans of the show delighted by its return, the series began to hit headlines outside of the TV review pages. Unsurprisingly for such a successful programme, it had suddenly become newsworthy. The coverage wasn't always positive, however, and the third series soon found itself in hot water.

It was noticed that Smeg fridges featured heavily in the show. Each workstation in the competition kitchen has a fridge emblazoned with a prominent Smeg logo on the front. Often there would be close-up shots of the fridges as contestants gathered ingredients and prepared to pull together their recipes. To the casual eye, this might not have seemed anything out of the ordinary. However, one viewer complained. Andrew Smith, of Manchester, wrote to the

*Radio Times* to voice his concerns, saying: 'The Smeg logo was so visible that I counted it 37 times before giving up.' He also complained that Smeg's website seemed to indicate a collaboration with *The Great British Bake Off* as it openly stated that it had 'once again teamed up with the show to supply six iconic fridge-freezers'.

This might not have seemed anything out of the ordinary, except that it meant the BBC's own guidelines were in jeopardy of being breached: product placement in any shape or form is strictly forbidden by the Corporation. BBC rules say producers must not feature products for cash or services, and any brands shown must be editorially justified and given limited exposure. The accusation that they were, therefore, prioritising a brand of fridge-freezer and giving it ample coverage in one of their flagship shows was particularly damaging. The BBC was forced to admit that it had breached its own editorial standards in so doing. They admitted to the fact that a loan agreement between Love Productions and the fridge-freezer company 'did not meet editorial guidelines'.

It transpired that the Italian firm behind Smeg fridge-freezers had loaned the £1,000 appliances at no charge for this latest series after being approached by staff from the production company. They had also supplied them for the two previous series. The result was that the comments on the Smeg website were requested to be removed by the BBC and a spokesperson for the Corporation issued a statement, saying: 'It is inevitable that some equipment will be seen in shot but producers are always looking to minimise product prominence. The independent production company had a loan agreement that did not meet editorial guidelines, therefore it is being revised and hire payments will be made.'

Despite this setback, the final was a triumph with record ratings for the show. *Bake Off* recorded a peak audience of 6.7 million and an average of 6.1 million – above and beyond anyone's expectations. It even beat shows on all the other main channels including *Holby City* on BBC1, which peaked at 5.1 million. And while Paul always knew there was something special about baking, he could never have predicted the success of *The Great British Bake Off* would be so enduring or wide-reaching: 'Who would have said Mary Berry, me, Mel and Sue in a tent with a load of bakers would have been the hit that it was?' he said in one interview with the *Sunday Mail*. 'You can't quantify that, it's just impossible. We peaked at 3.6 million in the first series. Series two, we had 5.1 million. This series we are around 5 million and that's before the final.'

Like all big reality shows, in the run-up to the big finale, fans wanted to know who had been crowned the winner. Nevertheless in the pre-final interview one journalist tried to get the information out of him. Paul remained resolute, however. 'I would have to kill you,' he laughed. 'My mother doesn't know or even my wife. I get asked about sponges, breads, cakes and pies and people will also have their own opinion about who should have been sent off *Bake Off* but "who wins *Bake Off*?" tends to be the most popular question I get asked.'

Nevertheless he knew that the overall reaction to the show was overwhelmingly positive. Not only were the ratings constantly heading skywards but he was frequently approached by would-be bakers who had been inspired by the show. He revealed that since he had been on *The Great British Bake Off* he had been sent hundreds of photos of baking attempts, as well as requests for advice over the social networking site Twitter. 'I get 20 to 40 a day,' he told one interviewer from the *Daily Record*. 'I do answer as many as I can. I'll say something like, "Looks good, concentrate on this next time".'

On top of that he was regularly approached wherever he went. 'It's on the train, in the supermarket, buying a train ticket, walking down the street, anywhere. Everyone is very chatty. Photos on phones have taken over from autographs.' And if anyone thought it was just women who were approaching Paul about their bakes – think again. 'Three Welsh international rugby players tweet me pictures of their cakes,' he revealed in one interview. While baking may once have been seen as the preserve and pastime of housewives, Paul was beginning to subvert that stereotype. Even so, he remained tight-lipped as to which famous rugby players had been contacting him. 'I'm not telling you who they are,' he continued. 'There's an English one as well. I get Scouse builders tugging my sleeve in pubs and asking me to critique them on their biscuits. You'd think *The Great British Bake Off*'s audience would be Middle England ladies and the WI, but in fact it's much, much wider than that.'

It was clear that *Bake Off* was reaching a huge demographic audience – far wider than the producers could ever have imagined. And as a result of the ratings success, there was speculation that the series would move to BBC1 now that it was becoming such a big show. Of course this would send both Paul and Mary's stardom soaring even higher.

It was a path well trodden by other shows that had debuted on BBC2 before finding success and moving to BBC1. *The Apprentice*, fronted by Amstrad tycoon Lord Alan Sugar, was one such example. And speaking at the *Bake Off*, a BBC source was quoted in the *Daily Mirror* in 2012 as saying: 'Viewing figures of 6 and 7 million mean a move to the flagship channel has to be looked at. The figures for the final are higher than the recent series of *Doctor Who* – even Karen Gillan's exit only pulled in 5.9 million.'

One thing that was certain was that if the series did move to the flagship position of being aired on BBC1, the producer would have the chemistry between Paul and his new best friend Mary to thank for the big move. Their relationship had cemented *The Great British Bake Off*'s reputation. While the show itself was a great concept, many were now realising that the success rested with the close friendship forming between the two.

# CHAPTER 9

# Greatest Judging Duo in History

It seemed the BBC had struck on a winning formula with *The Great British Bake Off*. The show's ratings proved that it was tapping into something that was in vogue the length and breadth of the country. Baking was now back in fashion and viewers – young and old, male and female – were all tuning in on a weekly basis to see what the competitors would dream up to help keep their place in the show for another week and edge closer towards that all-important final. Producers, BBC channel chiefs and, of course, viewers couldn't have been happier with what they were watching on their screens every week. It was the televisual equivalent of comfort food – inoffensive and warm viewing, fit for all the family.

But undoubtedly, the competition and how well the contestants were doing were not the only reasons why viewers were eagerly tuning in, week after week. Regardless of the impressive and creative baking being undertaken on screen, and the competitiveness between the contestants, one other very special ingredient was proving to be a significant factor why the show was such a success. It was the special bond between Paul and his co-judge Mary Berry that was propelling *Bake Off* to new heights in terms of its popularity. Viewers and TV critics alike lapped up the unlikely pairing's on-screen chemistry, which was plain for all to see. On paper it should never have worked: the rough and ready Northerner who had learnt his trade as a master baker working in bakeries in and around the Wirral versus the prim and proper doyenne of baking from another generation whose celebrity was cemented by her book sales in the millions and incredibly diverse range of products with an annual turnover of more than a million pounds. But for some reason it *did* work. Britain, it seemed, couldn't get enough of this dynamic duo.

As one astute critic in the *Guardian* noted: 'The success of their *Bake Off* pairing relies in part on these complementary differences: he the straight-talking Liverpudlian and she the kindly, rosy-cheeked grandmother we'd all like to have.' But something about the rapport between the two had everyone in Britain transfixed. Somehow the relationship – against all the odds – just worked. And television critics went out of their way to heap praise on the newly crowned King and Queen of Baking. In fact, the *Guardian* newspaper boldly declared 'Berry and Hollywood on *The Great British Bake Off* are the greatest judging duo in the history of reality television – it's their brutally honest diagnostic that crowns them.' The piece continued to shower praise on the pairing, saying: 'Make no mistake, Mary Berry and Paul Hollywood are *The Great British Bake Off*'s secret weapons. They're astoundingly good at what they do. They share a joyous enthusiasm for baking but, equally, their scorn can be unknowably ferocious.'

Other critics were quick to voice their opinions on the pair's dynamic, with Elizabeth Day from the *Observer* concurring. Writing about the partnership that has intrigued viewers up and down the country, she said: 'They make an unlikely double act and yet something about the two of them together just works. Watching them argue playfully on screen or in person is both entertaining and somehow reassuring, like eating hot buttered toast in a perfectly heated bubble bath.' And Judith Woods in the *Daily Telegraph* also picked up on the fact that Paul and Mary's on-screen relationship shouldn't have worked but it does, magnificently. She wrote: 'Hollywood shot to fame on *The Great British Bake Off*, alongside 77-year-old Mary Berry, a peculiar pairing that somehow, against all probability – rather like the almond and Roquefort loaf he sells for 15 quid a throw at Harrods – just worked. Beautifully.'

High praise indeed, especially when one considers that striking the perfect dynamic in TV judging partnerships is hard to get right. It's a formula that TV producers have constantly tried to work out over the years – with mixed fortunes. It's fair to say some TV talent shows have succeeded or failed on the basis of whether or not the combination of personalities on the judging panel has gelled. Ratings can sky-rocket or plummet based on this. And luckily, in Paul and

Mary's case, their contrasting personalities appeared to have worked a treat. As was often the case in TV judging partnerships, opposites appeared to attract. Despite coming from very different backgrounds and their lives having taken very different directions, their careers had converged and it seemed they were kindred spirits.

While many will find it hard to believe that the two had previously worked together before *The Great British Bake Off*, the reality was different. Paul first met his fellow judge eight years before being reunited by independent TV production company Love Productions during screen tests and casting calls for BBC2. Back then they were both working on the Good Food Channel, originally launched on 5 November 2001 as UK Food – a channel dedicated to cookery programmes previously broadcast on the increasingly crowded UK Style channel. The channel uses a large amount of programming from the BBC's archive. It resembles a former international channel run by BBC Worldwide called BBC Food, as both use similar content and have a similar format. The channel changed its name on 8 March 2004 to UKTV Food.

As part of the rebranding of all UKTV's channels to a unique name and identity, UKTV Food rebranded as Good Food on 22 June 2009, the last of UKTV's brands to do so. The name is based on that of the *Good Food* cookery magazine, published by BBC Magazines. The channel and the magazine continue to operate separately. When Paul and Mary first worked together, they were on a show called *Great Food Live*. It was a simple format, which ran through easy-to-prepare recipes that viewers could simultaneously follow with the live show at home in their own kitchens. Although neither of them stayed on *Great Food Live* beyond that series, they got on well right from the start.

'I was really glad it was her and she was really glad it was me,' Paul told the *Liverpool Echo*. 'I look after Mary. I make sure she's always got a comfy seat and it's not too chilly. I think of her like my mum and I want to make sure she's looked after. I think it's a Scouse thing. We're like a big *Bake Off* family. Mel [Giedroyc], Sue [Perkins] and I are like the naughty kids and Mary is our mum. She keeps us all in line.' For all the banter that the pair may have enjoyed on screen, as well as the various little scraps that they might have had over the judging process, it was clear from what Paul was saying that he had a deep-rooted respect for his on-screen judging colleague, who was fast becoming a close friend.

But certainly, while they may have been like a family on screen, their backgrounds and approach to judging were completely different. And as each episode was filmed, they appeared to embrace their 'good cop, bad cop' routine – with Mary decidedly playing the good cop. Meanwhile, Paul came from the school of judging attended by the likes of Len Goodman in the BBC's hit show *Strictly Come Dancing* or the *X Factor*'s Simon Cowell. He only judged the finished product and never minced his words. His blunt and to the point one-liners included: 'It just feels a little bit stodgy, which I wasn't expecting.' Meanwhile, compassionate Mary was always measured in her criticism. The worst you might hear would be: 'I'm really disappointed' or 'I don't like this at all'.

Journalist Sarah Stephens from the *Daily Telegraph* was invited onto the set of *The Great British Bake Off*. She observed the judging process with much scrutiny and picked up on Paul and Mary's rather unique relationship and different methods of critiquing the contestants' various offerings: 'The judging itself is fascinating to watch. During a technical bake (the round in which contestants have no prior knowledge of the recipes) the finished products are lined up on a table anonymously, while the bakers themselves sit on stools facing away from the bakes. It looks contrived, but it ensures no one can influence the judges. Meanwhile, Berry and Hollywood make their way along the table, commenting and tasting as they go. "This is over-baked," Hollywood complains. "Structure's all wrong." "Pastry's lovely on this one," Berry says, breaking through with her fork. Decisions are swift and definite.'

But for all that the pair's on-screen chemistry would cement the show's reputation, Mary admits they haven't always seen eye to eye. For one thing, she was adamant about refusing to be combative towards the contestants. She left that to Paul and wouldn't be drawn into it – it just wasn't her style. 'I wouldn't have taken part if I had been expected to make nasty comments,' she told the *Daily Mail*. 'The combative style of most TV competitions puts me right off. I don't see any reason to shout or swear or be hyped up. I want to encourage the contestants to bake, and people at home to think that they can make it too. It's not just entertainment, it's a giant cookery lesson.'

On top of that, the judging duo would often spend hours

deliberating over who stayed and who went from the show. On one occasion, it took them five hours to work out who would be cut prior to a semi-final in the first series. And their personal approaches to bakery meant they often clashed.

'Mary's angle is home baking, mine is professional, so we meet in the middle but with all the same passion and drive,' Paul told the *Daily Mail*. Although he admitted he'd learnt a lot from his fellow judge – specifically to use Stork margarine, which Mary had come to know after working for the brand during one of her first jobs in catering PR at a London-based firm called Bensons. 'I always used butter in my cakes before, but Mary said I should use a mixture of butter and Stork – you get the flavour from butter but the Stork sustains the crumb, making it lighter,' he added. Mary herself was quite forthright about the differences between their approaches to the judging process. 'Paul makes brilliant bread, and I've learnt from him, but I don't agree with him on lots of things,' she said in another interview. 'Paul takes a more professional line: every biscuit must be identical. It's not like that in real life; we're amateur bakers, and if there's one that's a bit of a wobbly shape or overcooked – not all ovens cook evenly – well, Mum has that one.'

It seemed their infectious line of banter – and the fact that they didn't always see eye to eye – spilt out into the many joint interviews they gave to the press during the time that the *Bake Off* was on air. In one interview with the *Guardian*, it was clear that they were enjoying poking fun at each other. 'He is difficult,' said Mary – with the interviewer noting that the way in which she said this was 'fondly, as if talking about a mischievous child'. Mary continued: 'But we respect each other. I would never argue with him over a loaf of something because he knows the science of it, how they've achieved it and everything.' Quick to put his take on their relationship across, Paul retorted: 'I'll argue with Mary over every cake she makes,' to which Mary 'rolled her eyes' before admitting that he was argumentative, saying: 'Oh yes, he'll argue with me.'

In another interview, their tit-for-tat conversations have also been played out. 'I think baking's far easier than cooking, and because of that it's more approachable,' Paul said, to which Mary was quick to reply: 'Rubbish! Honestly.' Not one to be deterred, Paul continued with his line of argument. 'Making a cake is one of the easiest things in the world,' he went on. Mary, the journalist wrote, shook her head vociferously and responded: 'He's very grumpy, isn't he? No, I don't agree with that. I think baking is very rewarding and if you follow a good recipe, you will get success.'

On screen, their very different judging styles are plain to see. In one meringue week on *The Great British Bake Off*, for example, Mary was not impressed with baker Danny's Monte Bianco, the dessert of sweetened chestnut purée topped with whipped cream. 'I am a little sad that I have not got crispness from it,' she said.

But while she may well have taken the softly, softly approach, Paul was much more direct. 'It just feels a little bit stodgy, which I wasn't expecting,' he said. He also told another contestant, Stuart, that his Chocka Blocka Mocha Meringue was something 'you could wedge a door open with', and 'even James failed to impress with his slightly barf-acious fig, chestnut, cherry and chocolate confection,' according to the *Daily Mail*. The newspaper noted Paul's immediate reaction, saying: 'Cue glittering ice-blue stare from Hollywood – apparently inherited from his maternal grandfather – and a look of baking doom.' He then continued with the judging, delivering his verdict. 'I don't like it,' he said, bluntly. 'Oh, you are brutal this week,' Mary told him.

But overall what made their judging partnership such a success was the fact that, despite their differing approaches, they could always find common ground. Fundamentally they knew that they both abided by certain baking principles and this meant they could be cohesive when they needed to be. 'But basically we think alike – we want to achieve the very best baking,' Mary said in another interview with the *Guardian*. 'It's got to be the right texture, the right flavour, it's got to look good, to tempt, the crumb's got to be right – everything's got to be right. And they [the contestants] also have to follow what they've been asked to do. But within that, they've got to be creative and individual.'

The truth is that a genuine friendship had formed between the two judges and they were getting on famously. Despite obviously enjoying teasing each other remorselessly when it came to their different approaches in the kitchen, the special bond between them was obvious. When the cameras stopped rolling, they would regularly socialise outside of working hours. No doubt the fact that both had been propelled to a new level of fame so quickly and so suddenly would have drawn them into an even closer friendship. Despite gracing the screen and bookshelves for years before, it's easy to imagine that the pair might have found their new status as a reality TV power couple slightly daunting, if wonderfully enjoyable. But nevertheless, having been on the *Bake Off* journey together from the very start, each would have doubtless been a great source of comfort and support to the other as they got to grips with the show's runaway success.

In fact, they became so close that Paul would often stay at Mary's pied-à-terre near Windsor whenever he came to London and needed somewhere to crash for the night. It's a sign that their partnership is 'absolutely genuine', as Paul said in one interview. 'Even more so off-camera than on. Mary is like a surrogate aunt. I often stay at her house when we're filming and she makes me breakfast and looks after me. We've reached the stage now where we can communicate with just a look.' And if ever there was a mark of closeness, it was the fact that Mary had entrusted Paul with the keys to one of her properties. In return for the favour, Paul regularly gives Mary lifts to and from the set wherever they might be filming *The Great British Bake Off* – so much so that he even joked that it was actually his full-time job. 'I'm not really a baker, I'm Mary Berry's personal chauffeur,' he quipped in an interview with the *Daily Mail*. The journeys – which would often be halfway across the country – would doubtless give the pair ample time to catch up on the busy goings-on in their own lives, as well as allowing them to discuss what they would be filming that day. And the fact that Paul would often go out of his way to help Mary out with a lift shows just how highly he thought of her.

And even when the pair were not shooting *Bake Off* they

would be sure to keep in regular contact. For example, when Paul went solo and started filming his own series, *Paul Hollywood's Bread*, in 2013 he made sure that he still found time to enjoy catch-ups with Mary over the phone. 'I like Mary so much,' he would tell the *Sunday Mirror*, with genuine affection. 'She is a national treasure and we do stay in contact when we aren't filming *Bake Off*. I often stay at her house and we speak a lot on the phone.' It was clear that this wasn't just a judging partnership that worked on screen, but one that permeated into the real world too.

Perhaps a true mark of their closeness is the very fact that Paul developed a nickname for Mary which he started to use when referring to her both on the show itself and while talking about her in press interviews: Bezza – a somewhat plebeian moniker, the irony of which would not be lost on Mary, who would regularly laugh it off. But once again, the fact that he would often, quite casually, refer to Mary as such proves how deep his affection for his co-judge really was. Over the following months and years as they continued to judge *The Great British Bake Off*, Paul would regularly refer to Mary using the nickname and often posted photos of them together on the social networking site Twitter, captioning them with phrases like 'Bezza and I'.

Making no attempt to hide his affection for the woman who he says is 'like my mother', Paul said in one interview: 'I always wore shirts and during the last series even had a jacket on a few times. But once I wore a polo shirt and Mary said she didn't like it, so that was it; I've never worn one since. Mary likes me in a dinner jacket when we go to awards ceremonies.

She reminds me of the Queen. There's something regal about Mary when she hooks her arm through mine to walk down a red carpet.'

There was one other moment in Paul and Mary's friendship that also made newspaper headlines. It was a moment that demonstrated both the judging duo's closeness and their – at times – polar opposite opinions on certain matters. After filming an episode of *The Great British Bake Off*, Paul decided he had a craving for something unhealthy; a little bit of junk to satisfy his appetite after a doubtlessly long day judging bakes and having to be on top form in front of the cameras. He told the *Radio Times* that he developed a hankering for salt after filming the episode and sampling the contestants' sugary creations. 'I crave salt,' he admitted. 'We recently filmed our Christmas special and on the way back to our hotel I pulled into a drive-in McDonald's with Bezza – that's my pet name for Mary Berry. I'd been eating cakes all day and had a big craving. "Big Mac, large fries, what do you want, Bezza?" She wasn't impressed!'

In another interview he gave a somewhat different version of events. 'I took Mary to a drive-thru McDonald's yesterday,' he said. 'Yeah, she loved it. Big Mac, large fries, six chicken nuggets, barbecue sauce, strawberry milkshake, a Dunkin' Donut...' he continued, obviously poking fun at Mary. She was quick to retort that she 'had nothing', before Paul interrupted and joked: 'And then she went back for an apple pie.' Indeed, Mary has always professed to being dedicated to healthy eating and exercise – she insists on eating only a light salad as an evening meal on days when she has been tasting cakes, and she enjoys regular tennis sessions with friends – so it's unlikely that she would have relished the idea of a McDonald's with as much gusto as Paul.

Their relationship, both on and off screen, isn't entirely uncommon. British TV has seen a number of judging duos whose successful rapport has kept viewers and critics alike hooked. On the *X Factor*, pop mogul Simon Cowell steered the singing talent show to an all-time ratings high thanks to his closeness with Cheryl Cole, who had replaced long-standing judge Sharon Osbourne when she left after four series in 2007. Their banter-driven relationship, coupled with the fact that the former Girls Aloud singer refused to take Simon's harsher criticism of the contestants lying down, meant that things often got fiery on screen – something that producers would have doubtless been salivating over. On top of this, there were also suggestions that Cowell was enamoured with Cheryl, despite being some two decades older than her – and denials to the contrary – but the often-flirtatious nature of their relationship meant that they became an object of fascination with viewers and tabloid journalists alike, always on the hunt for a new story.

Simon underlined the closeness of his relationship with Cheryl in a 2010 interview with the *News of the World*. At the time there was much speculation that there were divisions between himself and Cheryl and the two other judges on the panel – Australian popstar Dannii Minogue, sister of Kylie, and Irish boyband manager Louis Walsh. With no hesitation Simon admitted this was the case, going so far as to admit that the divide was due to his closeness with Cheryl. 'There are definitely two divisions,' he conceded. 'You've got Louis and Dannii, who look like they've been sucking on lemons. And then there's me and Cheryl trying to have a good time.' It seemed that he and his Newcastle-born protégée were just too close for the other judges to get a look in. 'Look, it's no secret me and Cheryl are best buddies. That is what Louis is angry about. Maybe I'm spending too much time talking to Cheryl and ignoring everyone else. It does get a bit like that some days because we're close. When I'm sitting next to her I forget everyone else. What happens is that the two on the other side of the table want to play as well. Well no, they can't!'

On other shows similar relationships have formed – such as the BBC's previous cooking hit, *MasterChef*. The series was presented by American-British gastronome Loyd Grossman for years before being refreshed when Gregg Wallace and John Torode were brought in to take over the reins. The pair had known each other for some 20 years; Wallace was a greengrocer by trade who first met Australian Torode in the 90s when he sold fruit and veg to Torode's exclusive restaurant, Smiths of Smithfield. They had kept in touch but had never worked with each other in TV, despite both making regular appearances on various shows.

But that all changed when the Beeb decided it was time to overhaul the *MasterChef* format and give the series the 'reality TV show' treatment, making it a lot more competitive and far less middle-class in its sensibilities. Their judging partnership helped to reinvigorate the show, taking it to record ratings. But unlike Mary/Paul and Simon/Cheryl, the *MasterChef* pair made no bones about the fact that they didn't have much of a relationship outside of the studio. It seemed that, although they spend nearly 60 per cent of the year together, as soon as the knives and forks are put down on the *MasterChef* set, the two go their separate ways. In interviews, they have admitted that they never catch up after work, or have even been to each other's houses. 'I have never been invited. Look, we go to work, we do a job, then we part company,' John said on Alan Carr's *Chatty Man* series on Channel 4. 'Usually Gregg disappears without saying goodbye but we do spend about 200 days a year together. That's enough. I like him but...' And Gregg agreed: 'You just can't keep that going in your private lives as well. We do share each other's problems. Well, I tell John mine.'

Obviously for the *MasterChef* duo, it worked much better to keep work and private lives separate. The pair also admit their differing opinions meant that they would often clash while on the set. 'Spending 200 days a year filming together, we got a lot closer, but any relationship where you spend that much time together inevitably gets strained. We used to fight about stuff, as we're both so opinionated,' John told the *Independent*. 'In the first series it was over [eventual winner] Thomasina Miers, as Gregg had said, "There's no way I want her." Then in the second round he said, "I want her." And I said, "You git, how can you hate someone vehemently one day then like them?"' Meanwhile, Gregg admitted that even when they're not in the kitchen the pair are by no means similar. 'John is aware I'm slightly OCD,' he also told the *Independent*. 'In the dressing room I must have everything in place. He leaves his clothes everywhere.'

It seems, then, almost impossible for all well-known and successful judging partnerships to work like clockwork all of the time. But so far, Paul and Mary had managed to make it work for them, both on and off screen. Soon, however, there would be something that would test their relationship – as it would see them spending lots of time apart for months on end. For a new opportunity would present itself to Paul, allowing him to take his baking skills to a very different audience in a completely different part of the world. He would be offered the chance to work in the US – but this time without Mary. So, was Britain's best-loved judging duo about to be split up for good?

# CHAPTER 10

# The George Clooney of Baking

Paul had managed to turn himself into a prime-time TV star perhaps when he himself least expected it. And it was all thanks to his passion and love for baking – something that he had dedicated his life to from an early age. But while his finesse in the kitchen may have propelled him to TV stardom, there was something else that would cement him as a true celebrity... the fact that scores of middle-aged women were seemingly falling head over heels in love with him! Suddenly it wasn't just the fact that he knew his trade inside out and could deliver incisive comments to the contestants on *The Great British Bake Off* that was sending his popularity soaring. Indeed, it was a lot more primal.

Female writers the length and breadth of Britain took to their keyboards to heap praise on Paul's vital statistics. 'Hot baker Paul Hollywood is making temperatures soar in kitchens all over Britain,' said the *Daily Mirror*. Meanwhile, Christine Smith in the *Sunday Mirror* swooned over him in a gushing piece, saying: 'With those piercing blue eyes and the masterful way he critiques a croissant, it's no wonder Paul Hollywood has become a bit of a sex symbol.' Another simply said: 'With such easy charm, is there any wonder Paul's become the housewives' pin-up?'

And that was just the beginning of the adulation. Soon his female fans would shower him with praise, both in person when they bumped into him on the street and on social networking sites such as Twitter and Facebook. One fan told him: 'You rock my world,' while another chimed in: 'You can squeeze my buns any time.' Others were more specific in terms of what it was that got their pulses racing. 'He's got eyes to die for,' one baking fan raved. 'He's so tasty,' said another. 'It's the way he stares at contestants so intensely when he is tasting their bakes,' added another devotee. Some even dubbed him a 'silver fox' – a term colloquially used to describe an attractive older man and, more generally, one who has gray hair and is often desired by younger women.

By the time the third series of *Great British Bake Off* kicked off in 2012, Paul's status as the least likely sex symbol was cemented. One writer, Jan Moir, even dubbed him 'the George Clooney of baking' when she was sent to interview him for the *Daily Mail*. The comparison is perhaps an easy one to understand – both men are experts in their field, adored by women, slightly older than the stereotypical male pin-up, and they easily slot into the sophisticated, suave 'silver fox'

*Above left and right*: Promotional shots of Paul for his *History of Bread* series in 2000.
© *Rex Features*

*Below*: Paul eyes up a triple-decker sponge cake, created to celebrate the Queen's Diamond Jubilee. © *REX Features*

Paul Hollywood and Mary Berry arriving at the Royal Festival Hall for the 2013 BAFTAs.
© PA Photos

*Above*: Even when they're not filming *Bake Off*, Paul and Mary are working hard to get people baking. Here they are shown talking breads, buns and bakes on *Loose Women*.                    © *Rex Features*

*Below*: *Bake Off* presenters Mel Giedroyc and Sue Perkins.                    © *Rex Features*

*Top:* Alan Titchmarsh welcomes Mary and Paul onto his show, which often celebrates the best of British food and drink.

A devoted sports car fan, Paul is pictured with his Aston Martin in summer 2013 (*bottom left*), and in the pits at Brands Hatch at the British Touring Car Championships (*bottom right*).

© *Rex Features*

*Top left:* Paul gives his famous kneading hands a workout on Sherrie Hewson's shoulders on ITV's *Loose Women*.                                      © *Rex Features*

*Top right*: Mary Berry with her husband Paul on the day she became a Commander of the British Empire.                                      © *PA Photos*

*Below*: Paul and Mary share a joke on Graham Norton's sofa while promoting *Great British Bake Off* on his New Year's show.                    © *PA Photos*

With Mary and Paul at the helm, *Great British Bake Off* has won a place in the nation's heart, not to mention BAFTA awards for Best Feature in 2012 (*top*) and 2013 (*bottom*).

*Above*: Paul seizes the opportunity to get a selfie with Mary and Pudsey the Bear at a BBC Good Food live show. © *Rex Features*

*Below left*: It's not every day you see a car like that on the streets of London, but Paul, an avid car lover, took part in the annual London to Brighton vintage car rally in 2014. © *Rex Features*

*Below right*: As well as on TV, Paul has had enormous success with his books, and he has had a number of bestsellers. © *Rex Features*

After a rocky period, Paul and Alex are now back together and in love.

category. Jan Moir summarised the way in which women were no longer just fascinated by the buns baking in Paul's oven. In 2012, she described him as 'an unlikely sex symbol' and went on: 'Look at him. He wears his shirt-tails over his dad jeans, his hair is gelled into porcupine spikes, his little goatee is frosted with grey. He trundles around like a Smeg fridge on wheels saying things like: "That's a good bake". Or: "It's got a good wobble". Or even, with a look of equal parts threat and regret when he espies the wan undercarriage of a luckless quiche: "Soggy bottom. You've got to raise your game."' As Moir noted, women seemed to absolutely adore 'the crumpet-making woman's crumpet' – 'Almost imperceptibly, like a hunky soufflé rising in the national oven of lust, the 46-year-old food judge has become a housewives' favourite. His fans call him the stud muffin silver fox, the new George Clooney and even – for those with spatula spanking fantasies – the Christian Grey of the baking world (after the millionaire in *Fifty Shades Of Grey*).'

As for Paul himself, his newfound status as a heart-throb was something he was quite shocked to learn about. After all, for someone who had only ever wanted to dedicate his life to baking, it was an unlikely feat. When Moir asked what he thought of the legions of adoring female fans, she says he was almost embarrassed by all the attention. 'Why have I become a sex symbol? I really don't know,' he said in response. 'Your guess is as good as mine.' Moir's take was that Paul 'shrug[ged]. He looks at his feet, clad in a pair of brown trainers. He is almost blushing, but not quite. You can tell that he secretly loves the attention – what man wouldn't?'

Whether or not this is the case it's hard to tell, but certainly dealing with advances from his hundreds, or even thousands, of female fans, became a second job in itself. As if he wasn't busy enough writing books, filming *The Great British Bake Off* as well as juggling all his other commitments and engagements, suddenly he was having to deal with offers of a different kind. In fact, in one interview with the *Daily Mirror*, Paul revealed that women were so taken by him that he was starting to receive marriage proposals. 'I get marriage proposals, maybe one a week,' he said. 'Women do flirt, yes.' In another interview with the same newspaper he admitted: 'I've had a few marriage proposals.'

Perhaps he had become more accustomed to the fact that women were throwing themselves at his feet by the time he conducted this interview because it seems he had finally started to understand why it was they were so in love with him. In typically modest style, he insisted that it wasn't because they were actually taken by him or the way he looks, but rather they were in love with his fame and popularity. 'They just want someone from the telly,' he told the *Daily Mirror*. 'They come and talk to you and I guess baking is more attractive and so they feel they have something in common with me. But I'm just a man from Liverpool. I enjoy what I do and if that gets people baking, then even better. I do think "Oh God" when people tell me I'm a sex symbol. It's very nice but I'm actually quite introverted!'

For Paul, who had always been a little shy as a youngster growing up (he told the *Sunday Mirror* in one interview: 'I was shy growing up and the persona goes with TV. It's not really me. I am quite quiet at home'), it would almost certainly have been a shock to be suddenly inundated with marriage proposals, flirtatious messages and to see newspaper columnists and feature writers clambering to heap praise on him for his good looks. But with all these adoring female fans thrust into Paul's life, it would be easy to assume that his loving wife Alexandra might have been bemused and perhaps even a little concerned by it all. However, when asked by the *Daily Mail* what his wife thought of all the attention, Paul replied: 'I haven't really asked her.' It seems they hadn't needed to acknowledge the fact that suddenly a myriad of adoring female fans were knocking on Paul's door. 'She just laughs at it all,' he continued.

He even hinted that if the legions of ladies who were so keen to get a piece of him saw him first thing in the morning, they might think differently! 'After all, [Alexandra] sees me in the morning,' he said. 'She has not really said anything. To be honest, we haven't really had that conversation. I think, as much as possible, we are trying to pretend it is not happening. I find it flattering, but a bit embarrassing.' In another interview, he admitted that Alexandra found the fact that her own husband had suddenly and out of nowhere become such an object of public desire quite humorous. 'She thinks it's funny,' he was quoted as saying. 'The other day two women walked past me and I heard one say to the other, "He's got the same blue eyes as that Paul Hollywood!"'

Paul's rise to fame and the subsequent adulation with which he was showered were not untypical phenomena, though. Even though he was a man in his 40s, and not your stereotypical pin-up, there was an increasing trend that saw men like him become unlikely idols for women. Suddenly, no longer was it just movie stars or football players who were the objects of women's affections. In the 90s this was always the case. Stars such as David Beckham, the former England and Manchester United star, and singers from boybands such as Boyzone and Westlife were the pin-ups.

Not only was it Paul who was enjoying this newfound status, but also other male celebrities in his age bracket, like the *X Factor* mogul Simon Cowell, fiery reality TV chef Gordon Ramsay and the risqué comedian Frankie Boyle. All were featured in various lists of personalities, having been voted 'unlikely celebrity crushes'. Indeed, Paul topped one such poll, which named him the number one celebrity 'secret crush'. He also found himself listed in another prestigious countdown – of the top 10 silver foxes alongside actor heart-throbs George Clooney and Trevor Eve, and football manager José Mourinho. Rather than embrace it, Paul sometimes seems to play down the likelihood of being a sex symbol. When asked about the accolades, he said: 'Erm, I don't believe it. It's flattering. It's very nice. It makes me feel a bit uncomfortable – I'm just a baker.'

Perhaps there was a movement towards women being attracted to men who were less preened and manicured, and more real – believable 'crushes' whom they might perhaps end up with. Writing in the *Daily Telegraph*, Judith Woods summarised this notion, saying: 'May I present to you, Paul Hollywood, Britain's most unlikely pin-up. Twitter is a-flutter, the racy opinions on Mumsnet would make a navvie blush and last weekend, when the *Daily Telegraph* included his Fifty Shades of Granary supplement there were practically riots in newsagents the length of the land. Let us consider the evidence: he's 47, built for comfort not speed, makes no effort to charm or flirt and is deadpan to the point of taciturnity. At home, by his own admission, he's partial to a bacon butty with white bread and pottering about in dressing gown and slippers – aah, slippers! Did you hear that, girls? Paul Hollywood wears slippers.' Woods went on to ask readers if the description reminded them of anyone, before breaking it to them gently that it was their husband, partner or 'that bog-standard bloke at the breakfast table. In slippers. Except better. Much better, of course, because Hollywood's shirt is crisply ironed and he is an artisan, which makes him sensitive, although possibly not to criticism, because he will still insist on wearing wet-look hair gel that hasn't been in fashion since Bros left the charts. But you know, somehow that lack of style nous only makes him more attractive.'

Of course the notion of celebrity bakers, chefs and cooks being an object of fantasy and desire isn't a new one. Nigella Lawson is a case in point. She is the self-styled Domestic Goddess, whose figure-hugging gowns that cling to her curves while she whips up indulgent dishes have attracted numerous column inches. There have been occasions when particularly vocal TV commentators went so far as to suggest that Nigella's seductive tasting, by licking spoons in a suggestive manner, verged on the pornographic. It's a bold statement to make, but nevertheless it shows the extent to which some cooks have been seen as an object of desire. And of course, in recent years, we have witnessed the emergence of the male chef as pin-up. Alongside Paul, there has been Channel 4's *The Fabulous Baker Brothers*, fronted by young heart-throbs Tom and Henry. Writing in the *Daily Mail*, Frances Hardy noted how their physical appearance – combined, of course, with their ability to bake – had made them a hit: 'A winning combination of skill, good looks, enterprise and the capacity to chat and cook with seamless fluency makes them ideal front men for their own TV cookery show. And, sure enough, The Fabulous Baker Brothers are now on our screens with their distinctive brand of hearty, blokeish and impeccably sourced grub.' In the same piece the two young men admitted that they had both managed to woo their future wives with their baking – proving, perhaps, that the way to a woman's heart is also through her stomach.

Another example of a chef propelled forward in his career – at least in part – courtesy of the fact that he has legions of female admirers is Gino D'Acampo. The Italian-born chef became a household name after regular appearances on daytime TV shows including *This Morning*, *Too Many Cooks* and the *Terry and Gabby Show* on Five in the UK. Fans up and down the country fell under his spell thanks to his 'heart-throb' good looks – a phenomenon cemented when he appeared on the reality TV show *I'm A Celebrity... Get Me Out Of Here!* His popularity was such that he was eventually crowned the eventual winner and King of the Jungle in the 2009 series of the ITV1 hit show. It was his personality and female fanbase, many said at the time, that ensured the rise in his popularity, and he was soon commissioned to write a string of cookbooks, as well as conduct live cookery demonstrations across the UK.

But in the same way that attention was given to Nigella Lawson's supposedly seductive style of cooking, Paul Hollywood found himself in the spotlight for, apparently, adopting a similar approach. His series *Paul Hollywood's Bread*, in which he taught viewers how to bake all manner of yeast-based products, hit the headlines after this too was seen by viewers and critics alike as verging on the 'pornographic'. The *Daily Mail* went so far as to say that he was creating a new brand of cookery show to get female devotees hot under the collar: 'As Nigella Lawson has discovered, a pinch of sex really can give your cookery show a lift. So when Paul Hollywood launched a programme about making bread he made sure there was no shortage of that particular ingredient. Some, however, might say he rather overdid the spice after viewers dubbed his show "patisserie porn". Despite his discernible paunch, the 47-year old master baker has emerged as a bit of a heart-throb. He had already established a legion of female admirers through his appearances on *The Great British Bake Off*. Now *Paul Hollywood's Bread* has helped cement that reputation with fans praising his deep tan, piercing blue eyes, and "sexual" way with lumps of dough.'

On Twitter, viewers seemed to agree. Joanne Macfarlane said: 'Is it me or is there something quite sexual about Paul Hollywood?' Another fan, Jenna Brown, said: 'I'm sorry, but how did he DO that? Malt loaf just managed to look SEXY!! I take my hat off to you Mr Paul Hollywood.'

In particular, they focused on the way in which he went

about creating his bread. While Nigella may have got attention for licking spoons, in this instance it was the manner in which Paul kneaded the dough that was under scrutiny. The *Daily Mail* added: 'As Mr Hollywood demonstrated a series of bread recipes – for a traditional bloomer, a picnic loaf, a rye, oat and ale round, a malt loaf and a rye and wholemeal trencher – viewers were treated to repeated slow-motion shots of him sensuously kneading dough.' The article also picked up on the fact that the segment's introductory soundtrack featured 'Whistle', a song by US rapper Flo Rida, which the *Daily Mail* claimed was full of lyrics – not played on the show – that make repeated sexual references.

During the segment Paul was quoted as saying: 'I use quite a bit of my body weight, down through my hands. It is a good workout – it gets rid of the bingo wings.' Indeed, when asked by one interviewer whether bread making is like sex, Paul replied: 'There is something in it. [*Bake Off* presenters] Sue Perkins and Mel Giedroyc get me to massage their shoulders. You develop quite powerful fingers kneading dough, so I'll do a neck massage and they'll go, "Ahh... ahh..." When they start dribbling, I have to stop.'

But for some viewers it was obviously too hot to handle, with the *Daily Mail* declaring: 'The programme's sexual tone proved too much for some viewers.' It also quoted Twitter users who backed up this theory. DistractableDaisy said: 'Hahahaha! Finally some cookery porn for the girls. Move over Nigella, Paul Hollywood is the KING of cookery innuendo.' Meanwhile, Andrew Nicholas said: 'Paul Hollywood: "play with it, stretch it"...bloody patisserie porn mate!' And Mathew Scott added: 'I'd like to know what tan Paul Hollywood uses! He's always glowing!'

On the subject of fake tan, it's possible that with all the attention, Paul might have become vain. After all, he would have been under constant pressure to maintain a certain look, to adopt the latest fad diets to keep his weight in check, or even undergo some cosmetic surgery in order to maintain a youthful appearance. It has been well documented that male celebrities as much as female ones have been partial to going under the knife and/or needle to keep themselves looking perfect while under the harsh glare of the media spotlight. Simon Cowell, for example, freely admits he has undergone Botox injections to maintain a wrinkle-free look while juggling various US and UK filming commitments with other interests. There have been other rumours that he has had more invasive treatments such as neck lifts, although the speculation was neither confirmed nor denied by Cowell's representatives. The media mogul himself admits that he has put himself through a rigorous routine of drinking healthy smoothies and that he undergoes regularly stress-busting exercises to ensure that the stresses and strains of being a primetime TV talent won't affect the way he looks.

Meanwhile, in 2012 Cowell's *X Factor* co-judge Louis Walsh has revealed that he paid £30,000 for a hair transplant, as well as forking out the cash to have the bags under his eyes removed. Louis, who has been a long-time friend of pop guru Simon, revealed at the time that he only decided to have surgery after jibes from Cowell. Louis was quoted in the *Daily Mirror* as saying: '[Simon] came up to me and said, "You know, you're starting to lose your hair, dear." I said, "I am not, dear. And anyway, you're going grey."'

Gordon Ramsay has similarly been the object of some tabloid speculation as to whether or not he has undergone work to maintain his hair. Some rumours were published in the now-defunct *News of the World* that he had put himself through a hair transplant operation in Los Angeles to maintain his luscious locks. Other high-profile male celebrities have also admitted that they too have done just that – including the Manchester United star Wayne Rooney, who paid for one such operation to curb his balding at a central London clinic in 2011.

It's an all too often recited mantra that must very quickly become written in the minds of male celebrities who find themselves suddenly propelled to fame from nowhere: if your face doesn't fit, you'll be replaced. So does Paul feel under any pressure to maintain his looks? Certainly not, it seems. When he decided that he should start dyeing his hair when it started to turn grey, it was his wife Alexandra who persuaded him that he should forget the idea and embrace growing old gracefully. As such, the *Daily Mirror* said Paul knew he had Alexandra to 'thank for giving him the sex factor'. 'About five years ago I did decide to start dyeing my hair but my wife forbade it,' he told the newspaper. 'She told me: "Don't you dare, Paul." Now I can see she was right. I think grey is cool. Sometimes you want a change but it looks ridiculous when you go back to grey.'

Then there is the small matter of keeping his weight in check. Many celebrities pay for the services of a personal trainer to ensure they keep in shape. For Paul to maintain a steady weight is certainly something of a challenge that goes with the territory of judging *The Great British Bake Off*, for the simple reason that he has to sample sweet and savoury bakes all day long during filming. His co-judge Mary insists that the only way she manages not to balloon in weight is because she just tries a little slice and sticks to eating salads for dinner.

While he was growing up, Paul managed to make sure he was burning the calories by playing rugby and hitting the gym, where he would put himself through his paces with a weight-training routine. But he freely admits that the constant sampling on *The Great British Bake Off* hasn't been good for his waistline. And after the first series of going all out and indulging in the amazing bakes (or *not* so amazing as the case might have been!), he decided to make a conscious effort to curb his portion sizes. 'I am big anyway,' he told the *Daily Mail*. 'I am solid. But this year, have you noticed I have been taking smaller slices?' One writer, Jane Moir in the *Daily Mail*, said that 'in person, Hollywood is built like a battering ram, with great, big baker's shoulders, a 44inch chest and nimble little legs'. But Paul insists his build comes from working in the baking trade from a young age. 'You spend years hauling big flour bags around. And then nine hours a day going like this,' he told the *Daily Mail*, making energetic and powerful kneading movements with his arms and hands.

Paul admits that he's not sure why he's such a hit with the ladies. While observers may speculate that it's because he's a regular type of guy whom anyone might meet while enjoying a night out at their local pub, he's less sure exactly why he's been propelled to such public adulation. Not least because, he says, when he was growing up and even in later life, he received no such attention. When asked in one interview whether he was as popular as a boy, he laughed off any such suggestion with his usual modesty. 'I was at an all-boys school and so I don't really know,' he told the interviewer. 'I was shy growing up and the persona goes with TV. It's not really me. I am quite quiet at home.'

Of course he himself had his own pin-ups while growing up, in the shape of screen siren Raquel Welch. 'Raquel Welch was my first crush,' he admitted in an interview with the *Daily Express*. 'I was about 13 or 14 at the time and I fell in love with her charms after seeing her in various films, including the sci-fi movie *Fantastic Voyage*. But my favourite was *One Million Years B.C.* from 1966 in which Raquel played a bikini-clad cavewoman. I did have the famous poster of her posing scantily clad in said bikini for that film on my bedroom wall.'

But while Paul hasn't let his fame or the adulation go to his head, he does his best to remain level headed when dealing with those fans who approach him. Fame, he admits, isn't something that he feels totally comfortable with. 'It is tricky. I was prepared for it, but wasn't ready for it, if that makes sense,' he told the *Daily Mail*. Whereas previously he was able to go about his own business without a care in the world, that is obviously different nowadays. 'I used to be able to go to the supermarket and do a bit of shopping on my own,' he said in the same interview. 'I still can, but it takes a lot longer because so many people want to speak to me.'

Even so, one commentator appeared concerned that as Hollywood's schedule got busier and with the prospect of working in the US on the horizon, he might change or plan a radical overhaul of the rough and ready image that had made him so popular in the first place. The *Daily Telegraph* wrote: 'We can only hope that, unlike Dan *"Downtown Abbey"* Stevens, who has become tanned and toned to the point of morphing into Mr California, our best-beloved baker won't be given an identikit makeover before he's even got through immigration. Because Hollywood, like his bread, is really rather special and there's nobody – nobody, I tell you! – we'd rather watch vigorously kneading our bloomers.'

At this point in his career, it seemed that no matter how popular, in demand or desired he became, Paul's commitment to flying the flag for quality baking and the respect he won from professionals and the public alike would not waver. However, unexpected developments in his personal life were soon to put this to the test.

# CHAPTER 11

# Baking For Blokes

After years of mastering his craft, it seemed as though Paul had finally managed to transform himself from a master baker into a primetime TV star. By his own admission it was something that he could never have dreamed would have happened, having told the *Radio Times*: 'This [fame] is an illusion. It's not real. It's superficial'. His first love has always been baking – anything else, he constantly reminds everyone, is the 'icing on the cake'. It seemed that no matter what success he enjoyed on the TV screen, what really mattered to him was that every day he was getting up and doing a job he loved – baking.

And while his chemistry with his co-presenter Mary Berry seemed to grow with every episode of *The Great British Bake Off* that was screened, TV producers were starting to mull over the possibility of Paul going solo. His popularity was undeniable. Not only did women appear to be throwing themselves at his feet in the streets, but the critics and newspaper feature writers couldn't heap enough praise on him either. It seemed he could do no wrong and it was only a natural progression that, while *The Great British Bake Off* was off-air, it was decided to give Paul his own show.

Of course, it would need to be different to *The Great British Bake Off* – producers wouldn't want to risk any criticisms of being repetitious. But with Paul's background there seemed to be an obvious treatment for the show: he would travel around the country, exploring different types of bread from various regions, and then explain how the viewers would be able to recreate them at home in their own kitchens. Like *The Great British Bake Off*, the series would be screened on BBC2, with the website for the show describing it as a 'series in which he reveals the secrets of breads from all over the world and shows how a humble loaf can be transformed into delicious dishes for breakfast, lunch and dinner'. Doubtless it was Paul's idea of heaven – the opportunity to explore, in depth, his love of bread and tell the world about it.

The *Sun* newspaper reported that the new series would be on screens in February 2013 and that it would be called, quite simply, *Paul Hollywood's Bread* – you could never accuse it of false advertising! It would, the piece continued, see Paul return to our screens and show him 'revealing some of his bakery tricks – but not just for bread'. Paul told the newspaper, 'I will be showing viewers how to cook things such as crumpets – and any recipe to do with yeast. I am excited about the series, it's going to be really good.'

And certainly the series gave a vivid insight into all the different types of bread you could find in the world. In one episode Paul visited an Indian restaurant called Kayal on Granby Street in Leicester. There, he was greeted by the chef Ajith Juman, as well as restaurant owner Jaimon Thomas, who, according to a report in the *Leicester Mercury*, put him through his paces. They taught him how to make a bread that he actually (for once!) didn't know how to make himself – a spinach dosa, which is often a popular accompaniment to a traditional Indian meal. And certainly Ajith knew what he was doing, having 18 years' experience of Indian cuisine. As far as he was concerned, Paul made an impressive first attempt at baking the speciality bread. 'Dosa is a very difficult skill to get right because there are a lot of things to think about – the heat of the surface, the mixture and getting it spread out very thin – but he did very well for a first time,' Ajith told the *Leicester Mercury*. Paul also won over both owner and chef with his courtesy and charm 'He was a great man, very nice, and it was a very good experience to have him and the BBC with us. It was a fantastic day I tasted his dosa and it was good. I watched myself on TV and it was interesting to see.'

It certainly seemed that Paul was winning fans wherever he went. For his part, he was inspired by his visit to Leicester, telling viewers on the show that the breads he had tasted were 'pure magic'. He told viewers: 'We have here a very good Indian restaurant called Kayal and they make some of the best-tasting bread I have ever had. Rice-based, lentil-based, flour-based, it doesn't seem to matter to these guys – they produce pure magic.' Viewers witnessed the painstaking process involved in making the bread too. Together, Ajith and Jaimon showed Paul how to re-create it by soaking a mixture of lentils and rice in water. Once the mix is soaked right through, it is put through a grinder before being left to ferment for six hours. It seems like a long time, but this is essential to get the flavoursome, fresh taste for which dosa is famous. Once you've played the waiting game, Paul said on his show, you then grind fresh spinach before spreading out the mix thinly and quickly on a hot place. On Ajith's version, Paul said: 'Wow, that's so impressive! The texture that you have got going on here and the smell – you can smell the spinach in there.' After being given this masterclass, Paul went on to make his own dosa while his teacher looked on with a beady eye.

The only problem was that Paul's version ended up too small because he did not add enough mixture. On the show he admitted to Ajith: 'Okay, so mine's not quite as dramatic as yours, but when it's served with coconut chutneys and a spicy vegetable samba, I reckon it will taste just as good.' It seems even a master baker doesn't always get it right, especially when he's learning new recipes.

Filming the show would doubtless have been a hugely rewarding experience for Paul. Not only was it an opportunity for him to branch out on his own without Mary by his side (though he would surely have missed his friend and co-presenter), it was also the chance for him to increase his knowledge of baking and master a few new recipes.

The masterclass in spinach dosa wasn't the first time that

Paul had visited the city of Leicester either. Earlier in the filming schedule for *Paul Hollywood's Bread* he had been there to make an episode on the delights of flatbreads. And if you thought bread was perhaps a limiting topic, think again! Restaurant manager Siby Jose said it was the second time that Kayal had featured on TV, after the Hairy Bikers visited in 2011. 'It is brilliant that we have been on BBC national TV twice,' he enthused. 'They have both been brilliant for us.'

Of course, regardless of the great content and the efforts that both Paul and his production team had gone to in order to ensure that *Paul Hollywood's Bread* did well, it all came down to whether or not the viewers would be tuning in. But luckily, the series was a huge success. After the first episode, the viewing figures were impressive. The 30 minute show – which had been produced by Love Productions, the same production team behind *The Great British Bake Off* – had 'risen to the occasion', declared the trade press magazine *Broadcast*.

*Bread* launched on BBC2 in March 2013 with an audience peaking at an impressive 3.07 million in the final five minutes, which represented 13 per cent of the audience share of everyone watching TV in that slot. What was particularly impressive was that it far exceeded the average audience for that slot on the channel. Usually around 2 million viewers would tune in, representing an 8 per cent audience share of all viewers watching at that time. Thanks to Paul's popularity, he had managed to top that average by more than a million viewers – once again proving that he really did have pulling power. What was especially interesting about the rating was that it beat the launch of *The Great British Bake Off*, which drew a still sizeable audience of 2.25 million after hitting the screens on 17 August 2010, which represented an audience share of 9 per cent. One can only assume that the new series did well because Paul had already appeared on *The Great British Bake Off* so viewers were keen to watch *Paul Hollywood's Bread* off the back of this.

The figures – which were provided by statisticians Attentional – had a clear message: Paul's popularity and power had grown over the last two and a half years. Now, despite the much simpler format of his new solo project, he was really pulling in the viewers, who were hanging onto his every word. The TV industry trade magazine *Broadcast* noted: 'The series is aiming to build on the success of *Bake Off* by capturing Hollywood as he shares his love for bread.' And it certainly seemed to be achieving this in spades. On top of all that, *Bread* was the third highest rated slot that night, sitting behind *A Question of Sport*, the long-running sports panel quiz show, which netted an audience of 3.02 million (that's an 11.9 per cent share) and the hugely popular long-running soap *Coronation Street*, which came out on top with 10.55 million (which equated to a 41.11 per cent share).

The BBC were obviously delighted. A spokesperson noted the impressive figures and also said that it was great that the series had managed to perform so well given the competition. 'The show peaked at 3 million viewers – and remember, we are up against *Coronation Street*, which is performing very well at the moment. I think the main thing is that it is encouraging people to make bread. You always hope that that will be the outcome, that people will try it and find out it's not as difficult as it looks.'

And if the ratings weren't good enough news in themselves, the critics were unanimous in their support too. Writing in the *Daily Express,* Virginia Blackburn noted the real appeal of the show. It wasn't due to the informative documentary on all things bread-related, it was the fact that Paul's devotees were able to see him on TV again! 'It's not really about the bread, is it? It's about watching Paul Hollywood make the bread,' she wrote. 'It's about a well-turned-out honey-glazed hunk rolling up the sleeves of an expensive shirt and plunging his big hands into warm, moist dough, and working it, masterfully. Surely it should be going out at least half an hour later, because it's basically porn.' Once again, it seemed Paul's status as an unlikely heart-throb was winning him even more fans.

Meanwhile, Sam Wollaston from the *Guardian* newspaper also spoke highly of the series. He noted that Paul appeared finally to be aware of his heart-throb status and was now using it to lure in the viewers. 'Hollywood knows his audience – practically winking at the camera as he lavishes attention on his dough like it's on a spa day, sharing anecdotes about his nan, and telling the viewers that kneading will "get rid of the bingo wings", the charmer,' Wollaston wrote. It seemed that while the beautifully shot half-hour series was acknowledged for providing a perfect insight into the world of bread, Paul's undeniable charisma as a TV presenter was what really shone through. Wollaston went on to conclude: 'Yes, there were stunning recipes and forays into history, but this show was mainly a seduction. He's even willing to wait two hours after a loaf is done, to let it cool, before devouring it. A gentleman, and a bread maker.'

However, there was one voice of dissent. Alex Hardy in *The Times* picked up on the fact that, without Mary's involvement, the banter and repartee were lacking. Hardy insisted this, in turn, meant that *Paul Hollywood's Bread* also fell a bit flat. 'It's not the same without the peculiarly appealing chemistry that runs between Paul and Mary Berry,' Hardy wrote. 'And it's certainly more blokeish. Recurring images of Hollywood eating with telegenic relish and murmuring sweet nothings of pleasure as he masticated certainly made the programme feel like it was designed to make us salivate – first and foremost. Perhaps this is supposed to engender the urge to cook, though it didn't work for me.'

And finally Keith Watson in the *Metro* also turned his attention to the show. He was all too aware of the seductive appeal of Paul kneading bread in a sensual manner: 'It wasn't hard to imagine the shivers of excitement rippling through a certain section of the population. "The more you play with it and stretch it, the better it will be..." said our host, Paul Hollywood, as he got down to business. The object of his affection was yielding moistly in his manly hands. "I use all my bodyweight and push down..." Yes, Paul! Yes!'

Aside from the supposed innuendo and possible sexual imagery that Watson appeared to be noting, he did acknowledge that the series showed just how passionate about baking – and, bread specifically – Paul was. 'Leaving the bad sex nonsense aside to prove for a moment – and Hollywood was clearly sending up his own surprise status as TV's Sexiest Baguette – it was engaging to see a man so enthused by his work,' he wrote. '"I need to start kneading," he said at one point, his bread habit clearly an addiction. As he pummelled and squeezed his way through bloomers and malt loaves, the giddy whiff of freshly baked bread started wafting up my nose. That's the power of suggestion for you.'

It's clear to anyone who watched *Paul Hollywood's Bread* that baking wasn't just a hobby for Paul, but a way of life – something he lives and breathes.

Watson remained cynical about whether or not the series' success would translate into an increase in the number of people taking up baking. 'Hollywood's mission to get us all baking bread is, I would guess, a doomed one. It just takes too long. But he'll make us all think we want to, so the book of the show will rise like an over-excited soufflé to the top of the bestsellers list.'

In fact Paul's love of bread seemed to be catching on. The TV series was a huge success by anyone's standards, but aside from cementing his reputation as one of the most popular TV chef personalities in Britain, it also achieved something else. Statistics showed that since Paul had been on our screens, the nation's love of baking was on the up. And specifically it was men who were becoming more involved in baking for the first time. Rightly or wrongly, baking was seen by many as a stereotypically female pastime – something enjoyed by stay-at-home mums with plenty of time on their hands. However, Paul had managed to challenge this stereotype. The preconception was to be slowly unpicked by the fact that a self-confessed 'bloke' like Paul was able to show how there was nothing wrong with alpha males enjoying whipping up a loaf of bread from scratch or even coming up with a sweet cake or dessert. It seemed baking was now something that both sexes could enjoy. Of course, this has always been the case, but here was Paul acting as a poster boy following his appearances in *Paul Hollywood's Bread* and of course *The Great British Bake Off*.

There was even research to support the notion that Paul's popularity had made baking more acceptable for men. A report in the *Scotsman* newspaper in Edinburgh published details of market research that showed more men were baking, thanks to his influence: 'Men are baking more after being inspired by TV chefs such as *The Great British Bake Off*'s Paul Hollywood, new research reveals.' It went on to detail the findings of the survey, which was published just in time for Father's Day 2013. On that special day, one in three Britons questioned in the poll said they planned to give their father some sort of culinary gift.

Research was carried out by the popular supermarket chain Asda, which found that sales of bread makers had shot through the roof by a sizeable amount since Paul's TV shows first hit British screens. A total of 27 per cent more bread makers were flying off the shelves, thanks to his influence. On top of that, the results showed that cookbook sales were up by 34 per cent – with many kids choosing to buy them for dad on Father's Day rather than the traditional aftershave, whisky or gardening equipment

But most interesting of all were the statistics relating to the number of men who were actually popping on an apron in the kitchen and getting their hands dirty. Retail analysts Mintel discovered in a poll that more than two-thirds of men – or more specifically, 68 per cent – were now regular bakers. Baking was something that men were now proud to be associated with. Interestingly, it was bread that was the most popular thing for them to bake – further suggesting Paul's influence. The statistics showed that almost half of men (46 per cent) chose to bake bread in the kitchen, whether it be white bloomers, granary batches or sourdough loaves, followed by 29 per cent choosing to bake cakes, 22 per cent whipping up chocolate brownies and, finally, 15 per cent baking scones.

And Asda were adamant that it all came down to Paul's influence, as well as other master bakers such as food writer, critic and former chef Simon Hopkinson and the Fabulous Baker Brothers, who were all becoming household names. John Cummings, who headed up Asda's baking division, said: 'It's great that more men are heading to the kitchen, rolling up their sleeves and getting stuck into baking – it's a well-known fact that guys love gadgets, so a bread maker or culinary gizmo is the perfect gift for Dad this year.'

But the research that seemed to suggest Paul was creating a new breed of men who couldn't wait to get baking didn't stop there. *Metro* newspaper also reported the trend, once again pinning it on Paul. The headline read: 'Woman's place is lying on sofa while he cooks' and it started: 'Celebrity chefs are freeing women from the kitchen and not because the girls are ordering takeaways to make time for heart-throb Paul

Hollywood's bread-making show.' It seemed Paul was helping to create huge social and cultural changes. The report went on to say that TV cooks such as Paul and Gordon Ramsay have inspired men to take a greater role in culinary duties at home. They had made it more acceptable whereas previously it might have seemed 'unmanly'. The report referred to a survey commissioned by Kikkoman Soy Sauce which stated nearly one in three women living with men now admit they are not the best chef in their home. A company spokesperson said: 'For years, the kitchen was considered to be a woman's domain. But it seems men are becoming bigger fans of cooking than ever before. Celebrity chefs have made cooking much more popular and it looks like this is rubbing off on guys. Cooking is no longer something reserved for women, or just a necessity, but can be fun for both men and women.'

The survey polled a total of 2,000 Britons and found that 34 per cent of women think their other half is the best cook in the household. Husbands and boyfriends are said by 36 per cent to be more likely to experiment with exotic dishes. And for 20 per cent of couples living together, the man cooks more often than the woman. The survey also found that more than 60 per cent of Britons say men now play a bigger role in the kitchen than in previous generations. 'It is great to see that both genders are sharing the cooking,' said the Kikkoman spokesperson.

Certainly no one could question that it was a good thing that more people, including men, were getting involved in cooking. But as his new series *Paul Hollywood's Bread* went to air, there was yet more research to suggest that Britain's newfound love of baking was directly correlated to the success of his new series. The Press Association reported that, soon after the first episode aired, retailers were reporting a huge rise in demand for home baking products.

Specifically John Lewis, one of the UK's biggest department stores, said they had witnessed a huge surge in customers asking about baking-related products. Sales of bread makers, they said, had shot up substantially the day after Paul's new series was played out on BBC2. Demand had gone through the roof, with sales rising by a staggering 132 per cent immediately after *Bread* was screened on the Monday night. And that was no mean feat, considering these machines are not always that cheap. According to the report, a bread maker typically costs between £35 and £189. Lucy O'Brien, assistant buyer for small electrical appliances at John Lewis, said: 'Sales of bread makers are up 132 per cent at John Lewis, with bread-making accessories up 60 per cent year-on-year. And with the new Paul Hollywood bread-making programme on our screens, we expect these figures to continue to rise.'

She added that the increase is part of a trend in consumer behaviour driven by the popularity of TV cookery shows: 'With cookery shows inspiring more customers to bake at home, sales of bread makers, stand mixers and food processors are increasing dramatically.' Meanwhile, another retailer also reported that sales of baking equipment were on the up, thanks to Paul's series. Over at Currys, a superstore specialising in the sale of electrical goods, equipment used to bake bread was also flying off the shelves. A spokesperson for the company said: 'I can confirm that sales of bread makers at

Currys are up 30 per cent year-on-year since last Friday.' On top of that, stand mixers such as KitchenAids and Kenwood K-Mix Mixers had gone up by 40 per cent.

It showed just how powerful Brand Hollywood was becoming. Not only was Paul a force to be reckoned with when it came to pulling in the viewers for his various shows but he was managing to affect retail trends too. No wonder publishing houses were eager to sign him up. It was a path well trodden by TV chefs such as Jamie Oliver, Delia Smith, Gordon Ramsay and Nigella Lawson. Often they would release books to coincide with a new TV series, with the book and the TV show being given the same name. It was a clever marketing strategy – the hope would be that the consumer might see his or her favourite TV chef whip up a recipe on the show and be sufficiently inspired to rush out and buy the book. And so it was no surprise that when *Paul Hollywood's Bread* the TV series was released, so too was a book of the same name.

But it wasn't the first book that Paul had published. Back in 2004, when he was far less well known and before *The Great British Bake Off* came into his life, he decided to release a book called *100 Great Breads*. Off the back of the *Bake Off* and his newfound fame a much simpler book titled *How To Bake* was released in 2012. The concept – as with all his books – was to teach anyone, whether they were a novice baker or thinking of applying to compete in *Bake Off*, how to bake a wide selection of recipes while aiming to keep them as simple as possible.

All three titles rocketed up the book charts, once again

proving his power as a brand. And that was about to be well and truly cemented, for just around the corner was a new opportunity that would categorically confirm that Paul Hollywood was destined for stardom.

# CHAPTER 12

# Paul Goes to Hollywood

It's a well-trodden path for any successful show that has pulled in the ratings on British television. After becoming a hit in the UK, the producers turn their attention across the pond to the lucrative, glamorous and hard-to-capture US market. And with *The Great British Bake Off* hitting the highs across the UK over the last few series, it seemed that it would soon be Paul and Mary's turn to cross the Atlantic. No doubt those behind *The Great British Bake Off* hoped for the same US crossover success of other programmes, such as the *X Factor*, *Pop Idol* and *Strictly Come Dancing*, all of which had translated into big ratings-winners stateside after first launching in the UK.

Pop mogul Simon Cowell, the brainchild behind *X Factor* and *Pop Idol*, saw his talent shows become some of the biggest on US TV after they were launched over there. While both series were lapped up by eager reality-TV show viewers, the success would also propel him from a mere judge in the UK to a superstar in the States. When each show went to air, Cowell would see himself emblazoned across huge billboards on the iconic Sunset Boulevard in Los Angeles, California, and while promoting them, he became a regular on the chat show circuit. He quickly became a sensation in the States, despite previously being relatively unknown. As TV's 'Mr Nasty', fans become hooked on the caustic put-downs and harsh one-liners that he would deliver in a cut-glass English accent, keeping viewers and critics enthralled. In fact, it's fair to say that many would tune in every week just to see how he would deal with a new raft of aspiring singing stars, all keen to make their mark on the music industry – many of whom, in the opinion of armchair experts, would never stand a chance of getting past the first audition.

After taking *American Idol* – the US equivalent of *Pop Idol* – to the top of the ratings charts for six series, Cowell then decided it was time to move on from the show, and instead launch an American version of his UK number one show, the *X Factor*. Although ratings, initially at least, didn't fare well in comparison with *American Idol*, the programme soon gathered in the popularity stakes, and by 2013 it was re-commissioned for a third series. Interestingly, Cowell was the sole judge from season one's line-up to remain on the panel. With millions in the bank – and just as many fans – it's fair to say that he was proof indeed of just how lucrative launching a UK show in the US could be for a talent show judge.

Of course Cowell was joining a host of other Brits to have enjoyed similar success after crossing the Atlantic. One example of this is Len Goodman and Bruno Tonioli. Since *Strictly Come Dancing* – the UK ballroom dancing competition show – launched, they had been on the judging panel. Len had acted as the head judge, having become a master of ballroom and Latin dancing during his career on the floor, and for years he had run a dance school in Dartford, in the north of Kent. A regular champion on the dance circuit, he was the perfect candidate to bring a measured, more serious tone to the often flamboyant show. Meanwhile, Italian-born Bruno, a professional dancer who had appeared in a string of music videos over the years, added the perfect over-the-top element to the panel. His exuberant comments, which often included wild gesticulations as well as him standing up from his judging seat, added a little bit of comedy and light fun to the proceedings, though his critiques of the performers' moves were no less savvy than those from his fellow judges.

The balance between Len and Bruno worked brilliantly. And, therefore, it was entirely understandable that when America came knocking for its own version of *Strictly*, these two stalwarts of the judging panel would be top of the producers' list to join the show stateside. Over there it was re-named *Dancing With The Stars* to reflect the format of celebrities being partnered with professional dancers, whittled down over a number of weeks until an eventual winner raised the prestigious glitterball trophy. The series became such a hit in the US that ABC, the network on which it was screened, took the bold decision to commission two seasons of the show every year, in comparison to the BBC, which had just one series that went to air throughout autumn and winter. But that left a tricky situation for Bruno and Len, as they were judging two shows, on different sides of an ocean, at the exact same time for six months of the year. Their schedule was gruelling – and they racked up thousands of air miles as they sped across the Atlantic between TV studios. At the beginning of the week they would film *Dancing With The Stars*, before hopping on a flight to London for Thursday, when they would go into rehearsals for *Strictly Come Dancing* before filming the show on a Saturday, then heading straight back to the airport: exhausting, but a perfect example of how a reality show crossing the pond can make stars of its judges.

And perhaps unsurprisingly it was this exact same phenomenon that Richard McKerrow, the producer from Love Productions in charge of creating *The Great British Bake Off*, was keen to replicate. In 2012, McKerrow stated that it was time to look at creating a Stateside *Bake Off* that would keep American audiences entertained, and maybe kick-start a revival in home baking across the pond. And after the success of the third UK series, an American version of the show looked set to happen.

A US network snapped up the rights after seeing the huge cultural impact that *The Great British Bake Off* had had in the UK. CBS – home to huge TV shows such as *Big Brother*, all-female panel show *The Talk* and *CSI: New York* – bought the rights from Love Productions, hoping to replicate its success stateside. McKerrow was expected to oversee the US version of the show, with suggestions indicating that it might simply be called *Bake Off*. In fact the initial reports that circulated in the British media proved untrue, and by the time the show got to air in June 2013, it was called *The American Baking Competition*.

But perhaps even more importantly, it would prove to be a huge moment in Paul Hollywood's career. Towards the tail end of 2012 there was much speculation that CBS did, in fact, want both Paul and Mary to remain as a duo and front the first US series, while continuing to film the UK version. The *Daily Mirror* quoted a US source in 2012 as saying: 'They [Mary and Paul] bring that lightness of touch that Americans would love. We are desperate for them to do it – and they're certainly top of the list.' But another insider told the paper that the baking duo's busy schedule – which included filming more spin off shows and an impending fourth series – could prove a 'stumbling block' for the negotiations. Nevertheless, it appeared that Paul was, understandably, in high demand with TV execs in the US eager to sign him up. But while they mulled over whether they would make a firm offer to Paul and Mary, they were doubtless considering how well the *Bake Off* format had done across the globe, not just in the United Kingdom. In fact, it had become something of a global phenomenon.

As with many shows that proved to be a ratings hit in the UK, those behind *The Great British Bake Off* saw the potential for taking their programme overseas. It's a well-trodden path by scores of other successful British shows, including *Who Wants To Be A Millionaire?*, *Weakest Link*, *X Factor*, *Big Brother* and *I'm A Celebrity... Get Me Out Of Here!* All of these shows proved to be popular with viewers on

UK shores before going abroad. And so the same happened with Paul and Mary's flagship show. *Bake Off*s are now being broadcast in Denmark, Sweden, Belgium and Poland, the *Guardian* reported in October 2012, while series were also in the pipeline in Ireland, Norway, France and Australia.

In Sweden the show was called *Hela Sverige Bakar* – which means All Sweden Is Baking – and garnered similarly successful ratings. In Mary's place was Sweden's own 'motherly' Birgitta Rasmussen, who had penned her own baking bible, *Sju Sorters Kako* (Seven Kinds Of Cake). But while Mary riled against soggy bottoms, Birgitta's bugbear was the 'dödbakade bottnar' ('deadbaked bottoms').

The format of each show remains the same, but the menu of bakes to be cooked up by the participants is tailored to the country's taste. Cinnamon buns, for example – which are so popular in Sweden that there's a national day dedicated to them – are the show's signature dish. Meanwhile, across the border in Denmark, viewers lapped up *Den Store Bagedyst* – or in English, the *Great Bake Fight*. The show has smashed all records for factual programmes on Danish TV channel DR1. 'This is the closest version to the UK original: if you turned down the sound, you'd never know the difference, though there are subtle pointers such as more Scandi wood, and no Smeg fridges,' noted Mark Cook in the *Guardian*. The tone of the Danish version is decidedly gothic, too. Mary's equivalent is Neel Rønholt, an excitable blonde woman, while her Paul Hollywood is a slightly older man called Peter Ingemann. Both, however, wear black in an attempt, it seems, to add a little drama to the proceedings.

In Belgium the show is called *De Meesterbakker* – or *The Master Baker* – and gets a withering review from Cook, who says the set 'really needs a visit from ITV's *60 Minute Makeover*. It lacks the jolly aesthetic of the UK version; much of the action seems to happen in a garishly lit warehouse, which means no tent, no flags, and no squirrels with giant testicles.'

While the UK's *Bake Off* action takes place in marquees, some of the Flemish version is filmed in the would-be bakers' kitchens, leading to 'an awful lot of clutter and mucky sponges you really don't need to see'. Naturally, with it being filmed in Belgium, the world's chocolate and waffle capital, both make regular appearances – and it only follows that the judge is one of the country's best chocolatier pâtissiers, Bernand Proot.

Down Under, it's no surprise that *The Great Australian Bake Off* has taken off with gusto. Australia's own version of *MasterChef* is as big as the *X Factor* in Britain after being given a dramatic makeover, and so it's no surprise that their *Bake Off* secured a primetime Saturday-evening slot. Regular bakes featured on the menu include national favourites such as lamingtons – a sponge cake covered in chocolate, dipped in coconut and cut into squares.

And it wouldn't be long before Paul was eventually confirmed for the US series. In March 2013, as preparations for the show started to swing into action, he revealed on Twitter that he had finally been selected as one of the judges. Taking to the social networking site, he said: 'The American version will be fascinating for me, don't know how they'll cope with me, mind!' By anyone's standards, it was a huge moment in his career: he was now on the brink of becoming a household name in the US and with that would come endless opportunities and possibilities for himself and his family.

To begin with, the inevitable financial rewards were tangible. Huge stars on reality TV shows in the US rarely bank less than $1 million for a series. Then again, such figures can go much higher if the show really taps into the public consciousness. Of course there would be a lot of hard work involved in the filming, not least because while he was busy taping *The American Baking Competition*, Paul was also contracted to film another series of *The Great British Bake Off*. Much like the globetrotting *Strictly Come Dancing* judges, his schedule involved jetting from continent to continent. Despite all the initial hard work involved, Paul was delighted by the opportunity to reach an even bigger audience. 'I have always said I would love to go to America, and with a name like Hollywood, it's perfect, isn't it?' he laughed in an interview with the *Sunday Mirror*. 'I'm very excited and I do think the show will translate well. It's now in 12 countries and repeated all over the world.'

On the surface the British and American versions of the show were very similar. In *The American Baking Competition* 10 contestants went head to head in similar challenges to those seen on the BBC2 version of the show, gradually whittled down to a final winner who was crowned the master baker. Except there were a few slight differences: first, there was a massive prize fund in the stateside show. The eventual winner would not only take home a cool $250,000, but he or she would also bag a cookbook deal – prizes that certainly didn't feature in the British version.

But perhaps there was one more fundamental difference. While it had been touted that Mary might join Paul in the US version of *Bake Off*, it was revealed that she had declined the opportunity because she was concerned about being away from her family for lengthy periods of time. The gruelling schedule of filming *The Great British Bake Off* while also juggling her other commitments made it almost impossible for Mary to start jetting between the UK and the US.

And so the producers decided to recruit another female co-judge. Enter Marcela Valladolid, a 34-year-old San Diego-born American TV chef and cookbook author who specialised in Mexican cooking. In the US she had risen to fame after presenting the Food Network show, *Mexican Made Easy*. And with her glamorous Latino looks and winning personality, she seemed an obvious choice. Described as 'a little less traditional than Berry', in pre-show publicity Marcela revealed that she was looking for bakers who 'think outside of the box' and who produce 'cool flavours' – something that she prided herself on doing in her own career.

Valladolid's interest in becoming a chef was first sparked when she began work at her Aunt Marcela's cooking school in Tijuana, Mexico. She graduated from the Los Angeles Culinary Institute as a 'Certified cook' and then moved to Paris, where she graduated as a classically trained pastry chef at the prestigious École Ritz Escoffier. On her return to Tijuana she started her own catering company and taught cooking techniques to classes of 40 students out of her home there.

Valladolid soon joined the staff of *Bon Appétit* magazine as an editor and recipe stylist. She also competed on the 2005 series of the US version of *The Apprentice*, in which she came fourth. Her first cooking show was on the Spanish language version of the Discovery Channel, which aired in the US and Latin America. In the series, she showed viewers how local Hispanic homes preserve and revive traditional recipes. Valladolid's first cookbook, *Fresh Mexico: 100 Simple Recipes for True Mexican Flavor*, was published in August 2009 and has since received positive reviews. Her second cooking show, the Food Network series *Mexican Made Easy*, debuted in January 2010. The accompanying cookbook was released in September 2011. Both the book and the show were shot in the city of San Diego – no doubt because Marcela knew the location well and felt at home there.

When it came to the series, Marcela had a clear purpose: she wanted to address preconceptions about Mexican cooking, in particular the notion that all Mexican cooking features yellow, greasy cheese. Instead, the point that she came back to again and again during the course of her series was that Mexican food was full of flavours and natural ingredients, not just processed food that you could buy at fast-food outlets. From there, Marcela went on to appear on other TV shows on the Food Network including *Throwdown! with Bobby Flay*, having been primed by producers as a face for the channel. Her youthful good looks, experience in cooking and passion for food all fitted in with the image that they were going for and she quickly became a key player in their scheduling.

Meanwhile, the US version of *Bake Off* would be hosted not by Mel and Sue, but by an enthusiastic, squeaky-clean, devout Christian comic called Jeff Foxworthy. Born in Atlanta, Georgia, he was the first child of IBM executive Jimmy Foxworthy and Linda Foxworthy, both of English descent – perhaps meaning that Jeff might know a thing or two when it came to Paul's favourite British bakes!

After briefly following in his father's footsteps and dabbling in work for IBM, Jeff went on to become an eminent comedian, TV and radio personality and author. Initially he found huge fame as part of a comedy troupe but went on to have a hugely varied and successful broadcasting background. The variety of different shows that he had become involved in doubtless impressed producers of *The American Baking Competition* in the same way that Mel and Sue were thought to be versatile enough to front the UK version of the show. In particular he was known for his one-liners, and during the mid 1990s he starred in his own sitcom, *The Jeff Foxworthy Show*.

His comedy troupe appeared in television specials and their own shows, while in 2007 Jeff hosted the light-hearted quiz show, *Are You Smarter Than a 5th Grader?* Between 1999 and 2009, he ran his own nationally syndicated radio show. If that wasn't enough, he was also given another show, *The American Bible Challenge*, to present – which ran for two series on the GSN network (Game Show Network). As far as the producers of *The American Baking Competition* were concerned, he had a clean-cut image that would appeal perfectly to the would-be audience of the show. On top of all of that, he has released six comedy albums, the first two of which went three times platinum. He has also been widely published as an author, writing several books filled with his jokes as well as his autobiography, *No Shirt, No Shoes ... No Problem!*

With the judges and hosts in place and ready to get started, the US show went into filming. As the transmission date for the first episode approached, by the middle of May it began to be heavily promoted on the CBS network. And it was obvious that the producers were keen to capitalise on handsome Paul's heart-throb status over in the UK. A promotional video on CBS's website titled 'Who Is Paul Hollywood?' interviews several British women on the streets of London. According to *The New York Times* they 'crow' over his good looks and 'strong hands'. One smiling woman observes, 'You'd like to be dough, wouldn't you, with Paul Hollywood? Who wouldn't? I don't mind him kneading me!' Clearly the producers were hoping that Paul's sex symbol status would translate across the pond too.

For a TV chef, there was no better place to make your name than the US, where food television has exploded over the last two decades. And it was stateside where the first TV channel 100 per cent dedicated to cookery shows was first launched in the shape of the Food Network. Originally the digital channel first hit the screens in 1993, fast becoming a firm favourite with Americans. It would take the best part of 20 years before it came to the UK and Ireland, eventually launching in 2009. Clearly it took a while for the appetite for day-long food shows to catch on with UK audiences. But in America, it seemed that viewers couldn't get enough of the increasingly popular channel, which screened wall-to-wall cookery shows of all descriptions, whether reality shows, documentaries, step-by-step classes for beginner cooks or for chefs who were at the top of their game.

The content on the Food Network is well structured to make it easy to understand for regular and would-be viewers. It is divided into two: daytime programming and evening or, rather, primetime programming. Daytime programming generally comes under the title of 'Food Network in the Kitchen'. The thinking behind this, it seems, is that step-by-step guides to cooking, along with simple recipes, are carried out by professional cooks and chefs. The aim appears to be that viewers can easily replicate these recipes in their own kitchens. According to one website they are 'instructional cooking programs'.

Meanwhile, the primetime coverage in the evenings comes under the banner of 'Food Network Night Time'. These shows are different in their focus to those that are broadcast during the earlier part of the network's programming. They include more entertainment-based shows, where the emphasis is on reality-driven programmes, cookery competitions, or even food-related travel shows. Generally speaking, they aim to rival the kind of programmes you might see on more conventional networks such as ABC, NBC and, indeed, CBS, where *The American Baking Competition* would find its home.

The Food Network has been a veritable success. In fact, few people could have imagined that, in recent years, it would be available in a staggering 100 million homes across the whole of America. The popularity of the network was growing exponentially, it seemed. One pundit said that on most nights, the Food Network would get more viewers than any of the cable news channels – no mean feat in the country that invented 24-hour rolling news networks. Interestingly, the Food Network was the brainchild and creation of Reese Schonfeld, also one of the founders of CNN – the original cable news network. It seemed he had a skill for tapping into the psyche of the American TV-viewing public's tastes and the next trends when it came to ensuring their appetites were satisfied.

The American food writer and campaigner Michael Pollan noted this phenomenon in an article penned for *The New York Times* and he came up with a theory as to why channels like the Food Network had managed to become so amazingly popular over the years. 'You'll be flipping aimlessly through the cable channels when a slow-motion cascade of glistening red cherries or a tongue of flame lapping at a slab of meat on the grill will catch your eye, and your reptilian brain will paralyze your thumb on the remote, forcing you to stop to see what's cooking.' Pollan concluded: 'Food shows are the campfires in the deep cable forest, drawing us like hungry wanderers to their flame.' The aesthetic appeal of great food being cooked up – the textures, the sound and the colours – was what appeared to be luring viewers to watch channels like the Food Network rather than others.

America certainly was the place to try to succeed, then, if you were a TV chef or cook. With the endless opportunities offered by channels such as the Food Network, as well as the more mainstream channels, it seemed that Paul would have a huge range of opportunities if he managed to achieve success stateside on *The American Baking Competition*.

CBS wanted the very best contestants for the show. And so, on 14 November 2012, they placed a number of casting calls advertising the show and inviting participants to apply. After a lengthy audition process that took place between 1 and 15 December 2012, an eclectic group of contestants was selected. They were Brian Emmett, Darlene Pawlukowsky, Effie Sahihi, Elaine Francisco, Francine Bryson, James Reddick, Jeremy Cross, Kolette Biddle, Whitney Beery and Carlo Fuda. The format was very similar to *The Great British Bake Off*. During the course of each episode the wannabe master bakers would be given three challenges to complete: a signature challenge, a technical challenge and a showstopper challenge. In the opening episode, the group were all asked to re-create an All-American Pie (technical bake), a Freestanding Savoury Pie (showstopper), and, finally, the most difficult of all: 36 Sweet Tartlets (showstopper). To say they were thrown in at the deep end would be an understatement!

There was one potential stumbling block for the producers of the show, though. Originally they had wanted to give the programme the simple title of *The Bake-Off*, but there was one problem: the choice of title had caused friction as the Pillsbury Company owned the copyright to the name. The bakery brand had run the *Pillsbury Bake-Off* for years, and bosses were concerned over CBS's decision to use such a similar name.

The *Pillsbury Bake-Off* had been a televised cooking contest, which first took place in 1949. Between 1949 and

1976, it was held annually before becoming a biennial contest from 1978. Originally the contest was broadcast on CBS, before moving to the Food Network and then finally finding its home on the Hallmark Channel after that. In recent years, it had been hosted by the lifestyle guru and business magnate Martha Stewart. Bosses on *that* bake off had felt that CBS's name was too close to their brand and requested they change it. CBS acceded and it was at this point that it was decided the new show would be titled *The American Baking Competition*.

Despite these difficulties, filming got under way in 2013 and the first contestants sweated it out as they vied for a place in the coveted final with the chance to bake for generous prizes and the title of Best Amateur Baker in America. Before long, CBS bosses began planning how they would ensure the opening episode was a huge ratings winner. It was vital that they captured the imagination of the huge number of Americans who enjoyed tuning in to competitive cookery shows on a regular basis.

Speaking ahead of the season premier to the Press Association, Paul said: 'I think it's going to be fantastic. They've got one in Australia that's being done at the moment. The Swedish one looks really good, and the French one is getting done as we speak. Long may it reign! If it's spreading globally then it's doing its job.'

He added that he thought the show would translate well to an American audience. 'It is a British idea but I don't think the theme is uniquely British. Yes, we go back a few years, but they do as well. A lot of their ideas come from Germany, Holland, France and Britain. [In the US] they've got a mix of everything and have things like the Mississippi mud pie and pumpkin pie. They're known for their baking as well, so I think it'll be a great show.'

With the promos rolling on the website and across the CBS network, the promoters made sure the series was advertised to as many people as possible. Everything was set for the first episode to air on 29 May 2013. But it would seem that even before the series finally aired, something would happen that would not only see the show hit the headlines in a huge way but that would dramatically change Paul's life forever.

# CHAPTER 13

# A Heartbreaking
# Twist

Well on his way to becoming a star on both sides of the Atlantic, it seemed life couldn't get much better for Paul. With an army of fans thanks to *The Great British Bake Off*, and apparently set for a hit with *The American Baking Competition*, he was at the peak of his fame and popularity. And to make that success even sweeter, he enjoyed a seemingly idyllic private life with his wife of 15 years, Alexandra, and their young son Josh. And as he flew to America, he would no doubt have mulled over the fact that he was on the brink of becoming an international star – something he could never have dreamed of when he first started his career as a junior baker in the Wirral.

Naturally, Alexandra and Josh would have been saddened by the prospect of Paul being away for weeks on end filming his new show, but it's equally fair to assume that, like any other loving family, they would have been eager for things to go swimmingly stateside. And of course Paul's legion of British fans would also be willing him on to enjoy the success that he so richly deserved. But what the fans could not have predicted is what happened next. An unexpected twist – and a heartbreaking one at that – caught almost everyone by surprise. On 17 May 2013, with just 11 days to go until the season premiere of *The American Baking Competition*, Paul hit the headlines for other reasons entirely.

The *Sun* published an exclusive in which they revealed that he had split with 49-year-old Alexandra. Their formerly stable relationship was over, it claimed. The headline read 'The Great British Break Off' and detailed the couple's shock separation, saying their marriage was over. But it didn't seem to be a straightforward situation. The piece went on to speculate about Paul's close friendship with his co-judge on the American show, Marcela Valladolid. The story began: '*The Great British Bake Off*'s Paul Hollywood has split from his wife after filming America's remake – with a sexy version of Mary Berry who got all dough-eyed over him'.

There was also official confirmation of the split from his agent, Geraldine Woods, who said Paul would be making no comment at this time on the 'private matter'. Speaking on behalf of both Paul and Alexandra, she added simply: 'Their priority is protecting their son.'

The *Sun* story came out days after Paul had arrived at the TV Baftas, where *The Great British Bake Off* had won the coveted Features prize, without Alexandra by his side. The newspaper detailed how he was now living in a studio flat in Kent, a short drive away from the family home, and also spoke of how astonished the couple's friends had been. Well known in their close-knit community, Alexandra was said to be enthusiastically involved in the church and the organisation of the local fête, while Paul had previously dressed up as Father Christmas for the children in the village during the festive period. Just days before Paul went to America, he and Alexandra were said to have enjoyed a romantic holiday in Paris, where they visited the splendid Palace of Versailles. This made their separation even more sudden and shocking.

Only weeks before the news broke, Paul had spoken of how Alexandra was not concerned about his new status as a sex symbol, further giving the impression that their marriage was rock solid. In an interview with the *Sunday Mirror* he declared: 'My wife finds it all hilarious. I get marriage proposals, maybe one a week. Women do flirt, yes. They just want someone from the telly.' He went on to describe himself as 'quite introverted' and 'just a man from Liverpool', giving an insight into his shy character and seemingly down-to-earth approach to fame. There was no sign of what was to come.

With little experience of negative headlines or tabloid intrusion, especially when it came to his private life, one can only imagine how Paul must have felt on seeing the end of his marriage splashed across the newspapers. The fact that it was coupled with so much speculation on his relationship with 34-year-old Marcela can only have served to make it even more difficult. Despite the speculation, he continued to remain tight-lipped and did not confirm or deny any romance with Marcela or that his relationship with her was anything but professional.

According to a *Sun* source, Paul and the divorced mum-of-one – recently voted one of the world's top 60 most desirable women in a poll – had 'hit it off from day one'. Before he flew out to Los Angeles in March 2013, she had described him as a 'handsome devil', while he called her 'brilliant' and praised her 'exceptional taste buds'. Following his return to the UK at Easter, the pair kept in touch via social networking site Twitter. The fact that they chose to exchange messages in such a public manner suggests they had little idea of what was around the corner. Her tweets included sending him 'big hugs from the U S of A' and asking if he was going to fly back to see her. In another exchange she declared herself 'officially the best mom/aunt/party-planner on the planet'. Paul joked back: 'I'll be the judge of that.' During March and April, while filming in Georgia in America's Deep South, the co-judges frequently posted pictures of themselves together on Twitter, documenting an apparent growing intimacy. It seemed the close relationship that Paul had shared with his *Great British Bake Off* co-judge Mary Berry was being replicated with Marcela.

On the day the story broke, Paul was filming the new series of *The Great British Bake Off* in Somerset. The following day he cancelled a book signing in Glasgow and a speech at the Scottish Baker of the Year Awards. It seemed that he wanted to keep a low profile while the tabloid storm rumbled on. And so it did; the speculation about his hitherto private life did not start and end with the *Sun*'s exclusive. At a time when Paul should have been eagerly anticipating the imminent launch of his career in America, instead he found himself in the midst of a media storm as more and more headlines were printed.

On 18 May, the *Sun* claimed Paul would be jetting back across the Atlantic to promote the US show – and therefore he would be reunited with Marcela. It seemed the press were scrutinising his every move, and doubtless this would have been a hugely testing time. The newspaper also used the apparent breakdown of Paul's marriage to revisit the splits of other famous celebrity chefs including Marco Pierre White, Heston Blumenthal and *MasterChef*'s Gregg Wallace, asking in typically tongue-in-cheek style: 'Why are chefs so saucy?'

Almost inevitably the Sunday tabloids were also keen to pounce on the heartache of one of the country's biggest stars, especially one who had previously enjoyed a clean-cut image and a happy home life. The *People* ran the first post-split photograph of Alexandra on 19 May. She was out shopping, not wearing her wedding ring, and had reportedly been staying with her mum, rather than at the family home in Wingham. Family members, including her brother Simon and sister Liz, were said to be comforting her. Talking about Alexandra's 'betrayal' at the hands of her husband, a family friend told the newspaper: 'She's been completely blindsided by this and sees it as a terrible betrayal and a real shock, which she is really struggling to cope with. This came right out of the blue. She couldn't have been more supportive over his career and was very proud of what he achieved. The fact he's going back to America now to turn himself into a global star makes it all the more sickening.' Meanwhile, a neighbour of the couple added: 'Alexandra has looked very unhappy the last couple of weeks and seems to have lost about a stone.'

On the same day the *Sunday Mirror* reported that Paul had been left 'racked with guilt' following the separation and – contrary to earlier reports – even suggested he was staying with his supportive co-host, Mary Berry. A friend of Paul and Alexandra told the paper: 'Paul is totally distraught and guilty about the devastation he is causing his wife and son. He has a very strong relationship with his son and he feels terrible about the pain he is inflicting by splitting the family nest. Alexandra is beside herself and can't believe he has done this. She supported him throughout the rise of his career. She would shrug off silly marriage proposals from potty fans. It was a massive shock for her.'

News of the split reached the *Daily Star Sunday* – usually more interested in scantily clad models and the latest football gossip – demonstrating Paul's wide-reaching appeal. The newspaper went even further than others, suggesting that he was planning to set up home in California with Marcela and her young son. But it was Alexandra's heartache that the *Mail on Sunday* concentrated on, offering similar details to the *People* and the *Sunday Mirror*, and describing how she had declined to comment when approached the previous day.

Meanwhile, in Los Angeles, Marcela was staying tight-lipped too. When approached by a *Mail on Sunday* reporter outside her brother Antonio's mansion in Chula Vista, Southern California, she was said to have 'smiled and shrugged, but declined to deny rumours of an affair' between herself and Paul. However, her sister-in-law Lisa insisted the speculation was wide of the mark, claiming: 'She'd find that very funny. She only has to have a sandwich with someone and they're supposedly living together.'

In the coming days further photos of Alexandra looking downcast and drawn would emerge. Scores of tabloid reporters and paparazzi camped outside her home, and the previous unknown – a constant but quiet and low-key presence by Paul's side during his rise to fame – found herself very much in the spotlight. Her gloomy expression and steadfast refusal to comment to the press suggested it wasn't a role she was comfortable in.

Meanwhile, a trailer for *The American Baking Competition* was released and said to showcase the on-screen chemistry between Paul and Marcela. In the footage a smiling Paul shows no sign of his inner heartache, telling viewers: 'I love being in America. I love eating cake, I love eating pie, I like eating bread, I like eating dessert, I like eating sponge. For me to land this job and be in America at the same time... I'm happy!'

Inside he must have been far from happy as more and more column inches were taken up with stories about his private life – and Marcela's. Events took an intriguing turn on 22 May, when it was claimed Marcela's own marriage had also broken up. The *Sun* reported that the star had split from her Mexican politician husband Fausto Gallardo – father to their nine-year-old son, also called Fausto – for a second time after remarrying him the previous year. The couple, who were childhood sweethearts, reportedly owned a plush home in San Diego, California, but were often forced apart by Marcela's filming commitments and Fausto's political campaigning in

Tijuana, Mexico, where he was running to be a councillor. A source close to the pair told the *Sun*: 'Her family were excited that this TV show was going to be her big break. But it's just been the break-up of her marriage. Some of the family knew they had been through a rocky period, but we thought that was past. They have kept it very quiet, and that may be for his and her career. They are both very driven people.' However, a spokesperson for Marcela later said that – contrary to the reports – she and Fausto had in fact divorced several years ago and never remarried. Nevertheless, it seemed they had at least enjoyed a short-lived reconciliation.

With so much speculation and all the parties involved keeping quiet, the exact truth of the matter was hard to determine. Clearly distressed by events, Paul was keeping a low profile. Supposedly in Los Angeles for a promotional tour, he did not appear alongside Marcela on US chat show *The Talk* – a CBS daytime show presented by popular host Julie Chen and also featuring *X Factor* judge Sharon Osbourne. Although it was not clear whether he was scheduled to appear on *The Talk* all along, it would have seemed fitting, considering how *The American Baking Competition* was launching to great fanfare, that he made an appearance. There were certainly a few raised eyebrows when he didn't join Marcela for an interview, especially as he was at the time in the US for promotional responsibilities for *The American Baking Competition*. His agent refused to confirm whether he had dropped out of promotional commitments altogether, but as Marcela gave interview after interview to plug the new show, Paul was notable by his absence.

No doubt keen to move on, he perhaps hoped that going into hiding would bring to a close the endless speculation and gossip. Unfortunately for him, he was very much mistaken. And along with the desire to stifle the headlines, any hopes that he may have had of reconciling with his wife were also fading fast. On 26 May the *People* reported that Alexandra was filing for divorce as she felt there was 'no way back'. She was reported to have spoken to a solicitor and begun proceedings. Whatever Paul's feelings about the end of his marriage may have been, any husband would be taken aback to read such personal news in the papers, especially given his close relationship with his son. As a relative newcomer to fame, becoming tabloid fodder was a world away from the previous quiet countryside existence he had enjoyed with his family. But professionally at least he needed to keep it together. Now back in the UK, again filming *The Great British Duke Off* in Somerset, he was believed to be staying in a bed and breakfast near Bath and leaning on co-host Mary for support during what must have been one of the most challenging times of his life.

It was at this point that Alexandra decided to break her silence. But despite the lucrative offers many in her position might have received or, indeed, accepted, this was no tell-all tabloid interview. Instead she simply took to Twitter for the first time since the split and revealed, in an understated message, just how tough it had been. Ironically tweeting under the name Hollywood_wife, she told her followers: 'I feel very blessed – when times are this hard, I've discovered what truly wonderful friends I have.' The following day she mentioned being 'back on kitchen duties', perhaps hinting at the fact that she and Josh were missing Paul's culinary expertise. Previously she had lovingly described him cooking his favourite steak flambé with prunes, cream and Stilton. After being flooded with messages of support from friends and followers, Alexandra went on to retweet several heartfelt messages of support, showing how grateful she was to be in people's thoughts. A look back at her profile showed that she tweeted on 11 May, saying it had been a 'different sort of a day'. It was just six days later that her marriage split was revealed.

Meanwhile, Paul resolutely continued to tweet about professional matters only, including giving tips on the perfect plaited loaf. He did, however, give the impression that he was less than happy with the media reports. On 23 May he wrote: 'Don't read them... They should all be in a literary fest for the best fiction!' And three days later he told another fan: 'I refuse to rise to the utter nonsense that's being written.'

But despite Paul's comments, the newspapers were still fascinated by his relationship with Marcela and continued to write about her. According to the *Sunday Mirror* she apparently told friends that she had no plans to live in England, and so any long-term union would have to be stateside. Previously unheard of in this country, the British public were clearly keen to know more about the woman who had supposedly become so close to homegrown heart-throb Paul. In the media she was sometimes portrayed as a fiercely ambitious character, on a mission to become the US's most famous female cook at any cost. Speculation over her relationship with Fausto and the pair's marital status continued, with the *Sunday Mirror* reporting that the relationship had been troubled for months but her friendship with Paul had proved the final nail in the coffin.

A friend of the couple told the newspaper: 'Marcela explained she had met someone who could give her everything she wanted. She didn't refer to Paul by name. All she would say was that the guy was rich and famous. Fausto had to go on the internet to find out who he was. He is obviously devastated but things have been on the rocks for a long, long time.'

Towards the end of May Marcela used Twitter to issue a 'shout out to all those hard workin' single mammas out there' and spoke of moving into a new home with her son. It appeared she was now most definitely single.

On 29 May *The American Baking Competition* made its debut on CBS, with the more cynical perhaps feeling that tabloid speculation over Paul and Marcela's relationship would at least intrigue viewers and boost ratings. They had had little interaction on Twitter in the run-up to the launch, beyond Marcela retweeting Paul's plug for the show. But whatever the state of play between its stars, the show launched to great fanfare at what should have been a time of great celebration for Paul. Instead, back in Britain, a photographer caught him looking strained as he arrived at the family home in Wingham.

Three days previously it seemed he had finally reached the end of his tether with the media. He took to Twitter to issue 'a personal request to the press'. It read: 'PLEASE respect my son's privacy he's had enough back off! I'm fair game but please leave him alone Thank you.'

Obviously feeling the pressure of the previous fortnight and concerned about the impact of events on Josh, Paul was snapped sitting in his car with his head in his hands. The *Sun* newspaper suggested he was at the house for 'crisis talks' with Alexandra, but again she took to Twitter to set the record straight. By now surely getting used to the almost daily press speculation, she wrote: 'Just heard via the *Sun* that Paul is coming for a "crisis talk"... Well he's got a bloody long drive then!' Alexandra was referring to the fact that she and Josh were on holiday at the time in a sunny foreign destination, believed to be Lysos, western Cyprus, the island where she and Paul had met and married. Previously she had asked her followers 'wish you were here?' as she posted a photograph of a large glass of wine. A few days later she posted another snap of some fresh fish and remarked: 'Got my appetite back at last.' She also posted a smiling photo of herself alongside the message: 'Fun evening at a very dodgy quiz night..!'

In actual fact, it seemed Paul was at the house to collect the last of his belongings while Alexandra and Josh enjoyed a much-needed break away from the glare of the media. But for Paul, there was no such respite. Once again he cut a lonely and troubled figure as he was photographed smoking a cigarette in the *People* on 2 June. The paper described him as looking 'dishevelled' as he puffed away in the street, before driving off in his £135,000 Aston Martin DB9.

But snatched photographs and the odd cryptic tweet aside were never going to be enough to satisfy the appetite of the tabloids. Given the regularity with which Paul and Alexandra's split had featured in the papers, it was only a matter of time before the *Daily Mail* made it the subject of one of the in-depth features for which it is so renowned. On 1 June, journalist Paul Scott undertook forensic analysis of the situation and wondered if there was any hope of reconciliation. Highlighting the cruel irony of the timing of events, the piece began: 'By rights, this should be a time of celebration for Paul Hollywood. After all, it is not every week your new TV show airs on one of America's biggest networks. And the Wirral-born celebrity baker has long harboured hopes of carving out the US fame to match his showbiz surname. Yet, instead of toasting his success, Hollywood cut a tortured figure this week as he sat slumped behind the wheel of his flashy Aston Martin sports car in a Kent village, his head in his hands'. It went on to describe how Paul had returned to his thirteenth-century marital home for 'crisis' talks with Alexandra, saying he bore the haunted look of someone who has come, belatedly, to the realisation that he 'faces losing everything. Gone is the carefree demeanour he displayed when appearing alongside Marcela Valladolid, the beautiful chef he is said to have become close to on the US version of *The Great British Bake Off*, which debuted on US TV on Wednesday night'.

The piece went on to offer what it claimed was an insight into Paul and Alexandra's marriage, with anecdotes from the past including his time in Cyprus where a younger Paul was said to attract attention. Scott continued: 'At the time, rumours flew around the expat community that he was being followed around by two besotted local girls even after meeting Kent-born Alexandra, who was working there as a scuba diving instructor. One British chef, who was a guest at the couple's wedding on Cyprus in 1998, said: "Paul was focused on his work. He was a brilliant baker. He helped open three hotels and worked incredibly hard. I never once saw him on the beach. It's hard on your social life, but Paul was always popular."'

The article also claimed to have uncovered 'new clues' in a bid to get to the bottom of the Hollywoods' marital strife, pointing out that the marriage had seemed stable until very recently. A month before the split, it said, Paul had set up a new business, PJH Media Limited, to funnel his growing television and media earnings. Significantly, he had appointed Alexandra to the role of company secretary. According to records at Companies House, the husband and wife were the only shareholders in the firm, which has its registered office in a terrace of commercial properties in Beaconsfield, Buckinghamshire. Alexandra was already the company secretary of his only other business, Paul Hollywood Limited, which was first registered as a company in July 2004. The new firm was set up on 7 March, just a week before Paul flew to America for filming. Scott's take on things concluded that the breakdown of the relationship had been sudden and unexpected. Surely Paul wouldn't have placed such responsibility in Alexandra's hands had he been intending to end it, he speculated.

Talk of Paul's financial affairs also prompted the newspaper to speculate about the potential impact of a divorce. As well as bringing up Josh, Alexandra had helped Paul set up his successful bread-making business, which supplies Harrods and Waitrose, suggesting she would be entitled to a sizeable sum should the pair make their split official and go ahead with divorce proceedings. The piece went on: 'Business is booming. As well as his six-figure BBC salary and a similar fee for the US counterpart, his bestselling book *Paul Hollywood's Bread*, released in March to coincide with a spin-off TV series, has pushed the baker's earnings close to £1.5 million in the past year. Accountants say that, even after a divorce, Alexandra would be under no obligation to resign her position, which, importantly, gives her a half share in the new company's profits.' The newspaper reported that Alexandra was said to be talking to lawyers, possibly about walking away with her share of the couple's assets, which included the £800,000, Grade I-listed home in the chocolate-box village of Aylesham in Kent.

Finances aside, perhaps most worrying for Paul and those fans rooting for his marriage was the suggestion that a reconciliation was not on the cards. According to the *Daily Mail*, Alexandra had rebuffed his attempts to make amends and took advice 'from her closest girlfriends at a spa day to celebrate her birthday', with some pals allegedly adamant she shouldn't take Paul back.

With almost every day bringing a fresh wave of press speculation about his private life, Paul's burgeoning career in America was perhaps furthest from many people's minds – his own included. The eagerly anticipated *American Baking Competition* had launched at the height of the media storm, but how had it performed in the ratings? And back in Britain, what was the reaction of the fans who had supported him throughout his rise to fame? Not to mention his close friend and colleague Mary Berry, the woman who had supported him through thick and thin. What would she make of this disturbing turn of events?

# CHAPTER 14

# Testing Times

With Paul's private life dominating the headlines over a number of days, it was no surprise that the public and a raft of prominent female newspaper columnists were keen to have their say. It seemed everyone had an opinion on his marriage split and the rumoured closeness to Marcela.

Leading the way was *Daily Mail* journalist Jan Moir, renowned for her no-holds-barred opinions and refusal to take prisoners. She is a previous winner of the Society of Woman Writers and Journalists' Lynda Lee-Potter Award for outstanding female journalism and the British Press Award for Interviewer of the Year. No stranger to causing a stir, Moir found herself under attack in October 2009 after writing an article criticising certain aspects of the life and death of Boyzone singer Stephen Gately, just six days after his passing.

Many felt the piece had homophobic undertones. It generated more than 25,000 complaints to the Press Complaints Commission, though none were upheld. The Crown Prosecution Service also concluded there was insufficient evidence that the article had breached the law. It did, however, lead to Moir winning Bigot of the Year at gay rights charity Stonewall's awards.

More recently Moir accused Welsh opera singer Katherine Jenkins of being 'fame-hungry' and surrounded by a 'thick fog of self-interest' after she ran the London Marathon for a cancer charity in full make-up. Jenkins tweeted in response: 'I adore and support other women [and] wish you could do the same', prompting many to take her side.

On 24 May 2013, under-fire Paul became the latest focus of Moir's attention. Beneath the headline 'A freshly-baked scandal and how fame can wreck any marriage', she suggested he had 'shed his family like a blancmange mould'. Speculating on his relationship with 'winsome' Marcela, Moir wrote: 'Now she [Marcela] has also left her own spouse – and seems to have become embroiled in a batch of not so glutinous-free baking. Clips of the American show reveal an undoubted chemistry between the unlikely couple: he the burly baker with the silver fox appeal; she the dollsized, doe-eyed salsa expert.' The piece concluded: 'Quicker than you could say ready, steady, barf, the man who invented patisserie porn had moved out of his marital home in Kent to a nearby studio flat. And we all know what that means. No mention of soggy bottoms from now until the end of GBBO series four, if you don't mind.'

Baking puns aside, Moir's piece also included a recollection of a meeting and conversation shared with Paul the previous year: 'I was struck by something he said. Which was that he and his wife had never really had a conversation about his becoming a housewives' favourite; a stud-muffin baking pin-up who was adored by millions of women. Not really mentioned. That was odd. Why had they not talked about it? One conclusion could be that even then it was already becoming a problem between them. Only time will tell.'

And suggesting that Paul's newfound fame must have played a role in the split, she continued: 'It is so sad, but we must never underestimate the hormonal folly of the newly famous middle-aged man. Of a husband who suddenly finds himself promoted from backburner to frontrunner; who becomes a flaming object of desire among young, attractive and determined women who are no respecters of his wife. Their behaviour might be just as reprehensible, but Paul Hollywood's flight from the home fires shows once more the perilous effect that celebrity can have in unbalancing a happy marriage.'

Moir was not alone in her take on events. Writing in her *Daily Express* column on 21 May, broadcaster Vanessa Feltz suggested Paul had 'lost his bearings'. Feltz was renowned for her outspoken opinions as a pundit and commentator. Having first risen to national fame presenting her eponymous controversial talk show, she became well known as a columnist and radio personality who truly spoke from the heart. Pulling no punches, she wrote: 'It's a truth universally acknowledged that a man with a few quid and a high public profile becomes infinitely more attractive to women. It's inevitable that he will feel flattered. If he has a particle of sense though he'll remember how happy he was with his loyal and loving wife before the trappings of celebrity kicked in and give girlies on the make a wide berth. Paul Hollywood doesn't seem to be blessed with level-headed common sense. It's a shame he didn't ask Mary Berry what she thought before he did a bunk.'

The *Sun*'s Jane Moore joined in too, writing in her column on 22 May: 'Let's hope it is merely a classic mid-life crisis and that, once it has blown over, he returns to the woman who loved him for who he was and not the "TV heart-throb" he became. However, one suspects that Mr Hollywood may be suffering from a far more pernicious, relentlessly stubborn condition from which there is little hope of recovery. He has started to believe his own publicity.'

It seemed no one was giving him an easy time when it came to this particular episode.

On the same day the *Daily Mail*'s Sandra Parsons had her say, suggesting Paul would struggle to win back the support of his female fans. She wrote: 'With one stupendously stupid move, *Bake Off*'s Paul Hollywood has destroyed his image and probably ruined his career. The reason we loved him was because he seemed so decent: sexy without being flirty, honest without being mean. We envied his wife, Alexandra, for whom he baked apricot tart on Friday nights "because it's her favourite" and fantasised about being married to a man who cared more about flatbreads than flat tummies. Now he's become close to Marcela Valladolid, his co-star on the

American *Bake Off* series – younger, thinner and to my mind far less attractive than stunning Alexandra, who manages to look gorgeous even when heartbroken. My guess is that it won't be long before he comes slinking back home, abandoned by minxy Marcela as she realises no one in America has a clue who he is. If he's lucky he may be able to resurrect his marriage and relationship with his 11-year-old son, Josh. I'm not so sure about his career – his legions of female fans won't forgive him.'

And so it went on – and not just in the tabloids, where outspoken opinions were the norm. Again demonstrating Paul's wide-reaching appeal, broadsheet journalists were also getting in on the act – and being equally damning. Writing in *The Sunday Times* on 26 May, India Knight felt there was a certain 'predictability' in Paul's marriage ending and suggested fame had sent him 'bananas'. Like Moir and others before her, she felt Paul's success – and his reaction to it – was to blame. She wrote: 'Now, obviously, it is entirely possible that Hollywood's marriage of 15 years was floundering before he became famous, and that his newfound celebrity served only to accelerate a separation that was already on the cards. But that's not how it looks. What it looks like is the latest in a long line of stupid middle-aged men who get their heads turned the moment they become high-profile.' And on the rumours that he and Marcela had become close she added: 'What is the matter with these men? It's the oldest story in the book and it's so boring. It doesn't matter whether they're on telly or working in the accounts department (though fame doesn't help). The story's always the same: been married a while, midlife crisis nipping at their ankles, waistline not all it might be, bit bored, bit comfortable, bit too cosy. They thought they were a sexy wolf, and they wake up in the morning and realise they're more of a sweet hamster. They love their wives – they cry when they tell them it's over – and they love their families, because they're not monsters. But it's so much more exciting over there, with the younger (though not always) model who hangs on their every word and never tells them to stop being a prat, take out the bins, or that this weekend is all about Auntie Gladys and her sore hip.'

On the same day as Knight, the *Sunday Express*'s Camilla Tominey published a similar theory. She wrote: 'The master baker has made the classic mistake all men of a certain age do when they enjoy their first taste of fame. They start to believe their own hype. Because a few sad women have started swooning over his piercing blue eyes and unparalleled kneading abilities, he's actually managed to convince himself he's the best thing since sliced bread. But just because someone in the press describes you as "baking's George Clooney" doesn't change the fact that you are actually a slightly overweight, married 47-year-old father of one from Wirral.'

But amid this barrage of criticism, one columnist wrote an altogether less detached piece, lamenting the actions of her 'blue-eyed baker boy'. Writing in the *Daily Telegraph* on 1 June, the formerly besotted Judith Woods admitted she was 'so upset' by Paul and Alexandra's separation because she had thought he was 'one of the good guys'. Not prepared to give up on a happy ending just yet, she signed off with the following thought: 'Let's hope Hollywood wakes up, smells the yeast and remembers which side his bread is buttered on.'

If Woods was anything to go by, it seemed even Paul's greatest female fans were disappointed and, despite their previous feelings, were finding it increasingly difficult to support him. But following the backlash identified by Moir and co, there was one woman whose support he could count on – the ever-loyal Mary Berry. According to newspaper reports, the *Great British Bake Off* stalwart had given her own take on events to friends and jumped to the defence of her co-star and pal. On 23 May, the *Daily Mail* wrote that Mary had reportedly told friends: 'You can't blame him, things happen and boys will be boys. If a boy goes into a cake shop he will try every cake whereas a girl will just stick to the one she likes.' The piece went on to claim that she had immediately phoned Paul after hearing the news of his separation, and that she had urged him to save his marriage by 'apologising and moving on'. According to the paper's source she had told him: 'My darling, I am here for you. Don't worry, we will make sure everything is OK.'

A spokesman for Mary, however, said she did not wish to comment. It was at times like this, though, that Paul could doubtless always turn to the co-judge who had become such a firm and genuine friend since they first started working together on *The Great British Bake Off*. Whatever the situation, no matter what may have been written about him in the press, he knew that he could rely on his mate 'Bezza', as he affectionately dubbed her, as someone to turn to during this difficult time.

As a result of her apparent show of support for Paul, not even national treasure Mary was saved from the pen of Jan Moir – although the columnist did concede that there was perhaps something to be learned from her. She wrote: 'Mary's remarks seemed like something from another century – which is because they are. Few women of a younger and more equal generation would ever claim that Paul Hollywood's behaviour was blameless – or to be indulged as just something that men do, so get over it. Yet 78-year-old Berry, who has been married for 47 years herself, also urged him to save his marriage by "apologising and moving on". The thing is, Mary's generation of stalwart wives simply did not divorce. And perhaps there is wisdom buried deep in her words of support; something to be said for weathering the storm of infidelity, rather than throwing a lifetime of love away.'

Perhaps Mary had another point too. Just as her 'boys will be boys comment' suggested, Paul certainly wasn't the first male celebrity to experience a marriage split. Nor was he the first celebrity chef. As both the *Sun* and the *Express* pointed out in spread-length features, he was just the latest in a long line of culinary stars to experience marital strife.

*MasterChef* judge Gregg Wallace has had three marriages – and all have ended. The former fruit and veg seller first got hitched in 1991, but wife Christine left him after just six weeks. In 1999 he tried again with pastry chef Denise and the couple had two children. But Gregg admitted to having 'loads and loads' of affairs and his wife later ditched him for cheating. In 2010 he married his third wife, teacher Heidi, who was 17 years his junior. The pair met on Twitter. But

Heidi left him and he has since gone on to date two other twentysomething women.

Nor has the path of true love run much more smoothly for Wallace's *MasterChef* co-star John Torode. After splitting with his first wife, the mother of his two teenage sons, the Australian-born chef found happiness again with second wife Jessica. But he left her and their two young children after four years of marriage and is now dating actress and former *Celebrity MasterChef* winner Lisa Faulkner.

Fiery *Hell's Kitchen* star Marco Pierre White had just got his first Michelin star when he married for the first time in 1988. He and wife Alex had a daughter, but by 1990 Marco was working more than 100 hours a week and the marriage was over. In 1992 he tried again with model Lisa Butcher, but within 24 hours he'd told her the marriage was a mistake. And then in 2000 he wed wife number three, Mati, with whom he had three children. They started divorce proceedings in 2007 but got back together, before separating again. Following the split, Mati admitted smashing up Marco's Range Rover and daubing insults in blood and paint on his west London home.

Seafood specialist Rick Stein was married to first wife Jill for 31 years. They had three sons and were business partners, with a food empire worth an estimated £32 million. In 2002 the couple split after Rick fell for his Australian publicist Sarah Burns. She was 20 years his junior. Rick and Jill divorced in 2007, and four years later he married Sarah. They now have two children together. Jill later said in an interview: 'Most of those famous chefs, they are on to their second marriages or they have got mistresses or girlfriends on the side. They all do it. I thought Rick had a bit more sense about him than that but I think he got caught up in the moment.' Echoing some of the columnists' comments about Paul, she said things had started to go wrong following the start of his television series: 'I always say that Rick traded me in for TV. You start to feel quite distant from someone when they're away, particularly when they're in different time zones. It's hopeless.'

And in the story perhaps most parallel to that of the Hollywoods, experimental chef Heston Blumenthal split with his wife of 22 years, Zanna, in 2011. They had met as teenagers, had three children and Heston had called her his 'soulmate'. He was reported to have left her after meeting food writer Suzanne Pirret, the so-called 'US Nigella Lawson'.

Tess Floyd, the fourth and final wife of late chef Keith, also had her theories on why chefs struggle to maintain relationships: 'The unsociable hours, women throwing themselves at your famous husband, being treated like a kitchen hand in your own home – it's a recipe for disaster. You must also accept that your house will be treated like a restaurant. I often found myself up to my elbows in giant, soapy pans because no chef ever washes up.'

Despite the precedent set by other celebrity chefs, fans were clearly surprised, saddened and disappointed to learn of Paul's split from Alexandra. As the *Daily Mail* reported on 24 May: 'Paul Hollywood won viewers' praise and support as the happily married presenter of *Bake Off*. But the celebrity cook is learning that a dash of scandal really can spoil the soup of success. Hollywood is facing the wrath of an unforgiving public...' The piece went on to quote former fans who had taken to Twitter to voice their disgust. One had tweeted: 'Pleaseeee don't say that Paul Hollywood is a love rat? GBBO will never be quite the same!' Another wrote: 'Paul Hollywood has ruined the GBBO. I'm so disappointed with him.' Internet forums were flooded with similar messages. Although there were also tweets and posts in support of Paul, many viewers were reluctant to forgive and forget. Could their feelings on the matter even lead to them switching off from *The Great British Bake Off*? According to the *Daily Mail*, the answer was a resounding 'yes'. A show source was quoted as saying: 'There has been a viewer backlash against Paul. A lot of fans on Twitter and other sites are saying they don't want him back. This hint of scandal has put producers in a tricky position because it is a really wholesome show. Whatever the truth, I don't know if people will look at Paul in the same way any more.'

In the following days, reports followed that the BBC were holding high-level talks over Paul's future on the show, concerned that his marital split and rumoured closeness to Marcela had tarnished the programme's wholesome image. Members of the team – including hosts Sue Perkins and Mel Giedroyc – were alleged to have turned on him for the same reason, though there was no evidence of discussion of this in public. But, once again, Mary Berry was reportedly determined to stick by her friend. An article in the *Daily Mail* on 27 May quoted a show source as saying: 'It's a complete nightmare. Needless to say the public reaction hasn't been good. *Bake Off* is such a wholesome show and it really doesn't help us. The team is split about 60-40 saying that he should stay, although it's all dependent on public opinion. Mary is the show and we know she has lots of high-level offers, and at the moment she is protecting him. If we sack Paul, Mary could walk and then we don't have a show. Right now Mary is his saviour.'

As the rumours persisted, it seemed things couldn't get much worse for Paul. But just days later the BBC intervened and put paid to the reports. A spokesperson for the Beeb said: 'There is no truth to the speculation that Paul Hollywood's position on *The Great British Bake Off* is in any way in doubt or under threat.' But despite the denial, sources at the Corporation told the *Daily Mail* it would have been 'nigh on impossible to replace him for the current series because filming had started when news of his marriage split and alleged affair broke earlier this month.' According to the piece on 1 June 2013, 'executives who have been in touch with *Bake Off*'s executive producer Richard McKerrow have refused to give private assurances to Hollywood he will still have a job once this series has aired this summer'.

For now though, Paul's career was safe – on this side of the Atlantic at least. In America, things weren't looking so good. *The American Baking Competition* debuted on 29 May but, unfortunately for Paul, sky-high viewing figures and rave reviews didn't follow. In fact, despite the hype, it got the worst ratings CBS has ever had for a Wednesday night debut. They were 23 per cent lower than usual for the time slot and the programme drew just 5 million viewers, compared with

10 million for Gordon Ramsay's *Masterchef in America* in a rival slot.

On website TVline.com the show was slammed as 'half baked' by Michael Slezak, who said there were too many contestants so you did not get to know them well enough to care. On another site, The AV Club, reviewer Phil Dyess-Nugent cuttingly wrote: 'This show is much more boring than it has any right to be.' He went on: 'Even for summer TV, this is one drowsy hour of television, doughy and shapeless as well as lacking in any nutritional value.'

Some viewers took to Twitter to criticise the programme. John Crook, a Los Angeles-based chef with 30 years' experience, pulled no punches, writing that the show 'insults the intelligence of every American home' and labelling the judges 'useless'. Another Tweeter, John McQueen, joked that Hollywood's name made him sound like a porn star rather than a chef, while Kristin Lueck said Paul was not 'recognisable' enough.

People also grumbled that they couldn't understand Paul's accent, with some even calling for the Liverpudlian to be dropped in favour of an American star such as Martha Stewart. Others argued that he lacked credibility because he was unfamiliar with US dishes and customs. And even the much talked about frisson between Paul and Marcela failed to provide any flavour, according to viewers and critics alike. The CBS website was hit by negative comments, with one viewer criticising the lack of chemistry between the pair. Stefanie Garfunkel from New York wrote: 'I had read all the stories about what may or may not have happened, and it was as if producers cut any scene of them going anywhere close out of the final version. They barely talked to one another and most of the episode was focused on the contestants. They spent a lot of time individually talking to camera. They actually lack on-screen chemistry.'

The *Daily Mail* ran their own review by Lina Das, who also highlighted the lack of chemistry between Paul and Marcela. She wrote: 'If talk of a close friendship hadn't emerged, one would have been hard pushed to notice much chemistry at all in the first episode of the series (somewhat unfortunately titled "Pies & Tarts"). Either through judicious editing or time constraints (the one-hour episode is littered with advertising breaks), the two judges don't even interact until halfway through the show.' Despite this, the *Mail* spotted a 'noticeable twinkle in their exchanges' when Paul outlined the contestants' second challenge, the technical bake. 'Are you comfortable?' asked Marcela. 'Do you think they can execute?' 'No,' deadpanned Paul, at which point Marcela was pictured laughing prettily. According to Das, it was actually one of the contestants, Francine Bryson, who 'appears in danger of fainting every time Hollywood opens his mouth'.

Essentially, Das didn't seem to think *The American Baking Competition* even came close to emulating the simple charms of *The Great British Bake Off*. Despite the similar format – 10 contestants going through the same three challenges (the signature, technical and showstopper bakes) – she wrote that 'the show's inherent Britishness and faint whiff of W.I.' was gone. She went on: 'The action is pacier, the pies much bigger and the icing virtually fluorescent ("That could bring in a plane from five miles away," says Hollywood of a particularly loudly decorated cake). Yet, somehow, by attempting to ratchet up the tension with fast camera cuts and aggressively competitive contestants, the U.S. version loses much of the bubbling drama of the original.'

Marcela too came under fire from Das, who she believed lacked the 'gravitas' of Mary Berry. As she put it: 'No amount of Marcela's perkiness can compare with the simple gut-wrenching drama of Mary biting into a scone and pronouncing: "I'm really disappointed."'

In fact, the contestants were about the only participants to earn praise from Das, who called them one of the 'undoubted high points'. She wrote: 'While British competitors may let out an occasional "Oh my giddy aunt", their American counterparts curse, slam fridge doors and cry – all within the first 40 minutes.'

This faint glimmer of praise was about as good as it got for Paul and the programme. Despite claims by the *Daily Mail* that the show's producers had been doing 'much to trumpet the pair's supposed on-screen sexual chemistry' including claims they shared a trailer during filming – *The American Baking Competition* had committed the ultimate baking sin in falling totally flat.

Only time would tell if the show would recover from its initial setbacks – and indeed, it would also be a matter of waiting to see how Paul and Alexandra's split would play out. Whatever the case, it was undoubtedly testing for all concerned. Though Paul may have felt going to the US was the obvious next move, and an exciting one at that, it certainly wasn't plain sailing. While he was now on his way to becoming a household name in America, he was also having to juggle some serious challenges. So, would there be a happy ending?

## CHAPTER 15

# Bread, Buns
# and Baking

Undoubtedly, Paul will have faced one of the most difficult times in his life with the break-up of his marriage to Alexandra. Regardless of what was written and reported in the pages of the newspapers and gossip websites, only the couple themselves know the truth of the matter. It would surely have been a hugely testing time as they struggled to deal with the heartache and disappointment at what had become of their relationship.

In the weeks that followed it seemed as if Alexandra was beginning to come to terms with the idea of what life might be like without Paul. In early June 2013 she took to the social networking site Twitter and wrote a poignant message in which she said: 'I've lived in a bubble all these years. I had no idea of the strength you need to go it alone. Single mothers, I salute you!' Clearly the prospect of having to raise Joshua without Paul being around as often as he might previously have been was daunting. Alexandra and Joshua had just returned from a trip to Cyprus when she posted the message, and the days, weeks and months ahead would be a tough time for the estranged couple. Reports suggested that Alexandra intended to go ahead with a full divorce, and that she had consulted lawyers on the best way to proceed. Only time would tell exactly how matters would conclude.

For his part, Paul was doing his best to put on a brave face and even managed to see the funny side of the media storm that had engulfed him ever since the news of his separation from Alexandra broke. He was taking part in a demonstration at the BBC Good Food Show at Birmingham's NEC Arena alongside *Great British Bake Off* quarter-finalist Cathryn Dresser. Over the years he has been regularly involved in cookery demonstrations – some on a smaller scale, others like the BBC Good Food Show, which is a huge annual event attended by thousands of food lovers in order to catch a glimpse of their favourite chefs cooking up exciting dishes and to learn about new ingredients, techniques and gadgets. During the demonstration he quipped: 'This is the kind of bread that will get you recognised. I should know, I've had a lot of publicity recently,' before giving what the *Sun* reported to be a 'cheeky wink' at the 400-strong audience. At least he was making the best of a tricky situation.

While he was kept busy with his hectic work schedule, Paul had obviously decided that he needed some respite from the glare of the media spotlight. For a bit of downtime, he turned to one of his first loves and on this occasion it had nothing to do with baking. As the press reported the on-going drama of his love life, Paul was photographed at a car fair in the north of England. Photographers snapped him eyeing up luxury cars at the annual Cholmondeley Pageant of Power in Cheshire. Despite everything he must have been feeling, he looked as though he was enjoying himself as he jumped in and out of sports cars and top-of-the-range vehicles at the smart festival. Paul had made no secret of the fact that he adored anything on wheels that could go fast. It was a passion that he had discovered while living in Cyprus when he developed a love of super biking – and now it seemed that his passion for fast engines had become a full-blown love affair. In an interview with the *Daily Mail*, he described his love for fast cars: 'I've had a lot of Jaguars and Range Rovers, Lotus Esprit Turbos... I've been into cars all my life,' he told the reporter. 'Aston Martin employs people here, they're British, they're Bond, so when I got my DB9 it was a very special day. I'll be paying for it for the rest of my life, but it was something I'd wanted since I had a DB5 poster on my wall.' He went on to reveal that the hairs on his neck were standing up as he drove it to his mother's house, before adding: 'She said, "Don't go straight back home, let's go past my friend's house." The noise of the engine tends to get the curtains twitching, but we had to go past four times before she looked out!'

And it seemed his newfound celebrity meant that Paul was being given access to some top-of-the-range vehicles that he might never have dreamt of getting his hands on. 'Aston Martin now lends me its new cars to try,' he said in the same interview. 'I had a Rapide for about two months, and for CarFest last summer I took down a V12 Vantage GT3, which is technically a racing car. The one I've brought here is the brand new Vanquish. It's got the best interior I've ever seen, all touch controls. I think it does close to 200mph, and around the rural little roads near me I managed to open the taps and see what it was like on the corners. It was very, very good. I'm still getting used to it, but it might be my favourite Aston ever.'

Meanwhile in another interview, this time with the *Sunday Express*, Paul said that his weakness was 'cakes and cars' – which neatly sums up where his passions lie. He elaborated: 'If I see a nice car I've got to get into it. I end up stopping at a lot of showrooms. If I could pass any law, it would be to fine people who only drive in the middle lane of the motorway. I drive an Aston Martin. It's a beautiful car and very British, manufactured in this country. The shop I can't walk into is cars.'

It was even reported in various national newspapers that to help put his 'marital woes' behind him, Paul splashed out on a new Aston Martin in the summer of 2013. The *MailOnline* website said that Paul 'wasted no time in stepping out and about in his new motor' and that he 'was spotted taking the car for a spin near his home'. Paul was obviously indulging his love for the swanky motor while simultaneously showing his support of British manufacturing, and perhaps taking an opportunity to forget about the drama surrounding his personal life while putting the new motor through its paces.

However, at this time Alexandra was still possibly struggling to come to terms with what had happened. It all started after Paul had tweeted a pictured of an empty plate, having enjoyed a meal with another dining companion. Many people speculated that it was Marcela, although it is impossible to know for definite. Paul accompanied the picture with the message: 'Great meal. Ahhh x'. But it seemed that Alexandra would use the seemingly innocent message to poke fun at her estranged husband. Hours later, Alexandra posted a message to her more than 2,000 followers, saying: 'I have to say, if I went out on a romantic evening I'd be gazing lovingly at my date, not tweeting my empty plate... What do you think girls?' She had also recently changed her Twitter profile to say that she was 'soon to belong to The First Wives Club'. Her flock of online supporters – whom Alexandra referred to as her 'sisterhood' – soon came back with loads of messages of support.

This wasn't the first time that Alexandra had alluded to Paul and his co-presenter Marcela on Twitter. In another apparent clash Marcela had posted a picture of herself sitting on a step in a low-cut dress with the caption: '#waiting #patiently #astheworldrushesby.' Alexandra quickly posted a picture of herself sitting down with her finger curiously placed on her mouth with the caption: '#waiting #patiently #astheworldrushesby ... ahhh but waiting for whom, I wonder?'

But that wasn't the end of it. It seemed that Alexandra was determined to tell her side of the story. No doubt she would have had scores of journalists knocking on her door since the news of the split became public, offering her vast quantities of money and using all of their persuasive powers to try to convince her to give an account of her version of events. For a long time Alexandra resolutely kept her lips sealed (apart from, of course, the occasional wry comment on Twitter). But in July 2013, something changed. Whether she had just grown tired of being contacted by the media and wanted to do something to draw a line under events, or she genuinely wanted to tell her side of the story, Alexandra decided to give a tell-all interview about her relationship – and its disintegration – to a major national newspaper.

The interview ran across two double pages in the *Daily Mail*, laying bare Alexandra's grief and devastation over the end of her marriage to Paul. Throughout the interview Alexandra was said to regularly break down in tears as she recounted her past relationship with Paul and spoke about where it all went wrong. It made for gripping reading. The newspaper reported the fact that Alexandra had filed for divorce on the basis of Paul's adultery and that Paul was not contesting this.

Alexandra insisted that she and Paul had agreed not to go into the specifics of the events leading up to their split, in order to protect Joshua. After all, it would have made for difficult reading for Joshua once he grew up to read any press clippings.

But it was clear from what Alexandra said in the course of her interview that the split had come suddenly and only after Paul's spell filming *The American Baking Competition* in the US. It was also clear that Alexandra was heartbroken by how her seemingly idyllic life had suddenly and very dramatically unfolded.

'I felt very secure with Paul. I trusted him completely. I loved him and he loved me. We were happy and life was good,' Alexandra told interviewer Helen Weathers. 'Friends would say to me, usually after they'd finished one of Paul's fabulous puddings: "How wonderful, you lucky girl." And, yes, I did feel incredibly lucky. Paul was the loveliest of husbands and a brilliant father. I used to laugh when people called him a sex symbol because to me he was just my husband. He was the same Paul he'd always been. He was very grounded. Fame didn't go to his head at all.'

Despite admitting that Paul was still the great love of her life, Alexandra insisted there was no chance of reconciliation. 'I love my husband and I was and still am very proud of what he has achieved, but there is no going back and I just want this finished with and to move on,' she said in the interview. 'I don't know if he still loves me. I'd like to think there's always going to be some affection there. You can't share 15 years of marriage and not have anything left, but right now I just don't know.'

What appeared most shocking of all for Alexandra was the fact that it had all happened so quickly and without any warning. 'In the space of four weeks my life changed irrevocably,' she said. 'One minute I was happily married and the next I wasn't. It was a complete shock. I still haven't completely absorbed it yet.'

Moreover, it was also obvious that the split was affecting Alexandra's health, too. She admitted in the interview that her usual love of cooking had dried up in the aftermath of the separation and she had lost a staggering two stone in weight.

'Sometimes I wake up in the morning and can't believe it's happened,' he said. 'I feel utterly bewildered and incredibly sad. Paul went to America and when he came back everything was different, everything had changed. He is a very decisive person. What you see on the *Bake Off* is Paul. He will say it as it is. If he likes something, he will say it; if he doesn't like it, he will say it. That's him.'

Considering everything that Alexandra had been through owing to the separation and subsequent break-up of their small family, one might imagine that she must have feelings of anger, bitterness and desire for revenge. Not so. It's testament to the loving woman she is that she managed to set aside any feelings of anger towards Paul in the immediate aftermath of their split and say that she hoped the public didn't turn against her husband. 'After we split up, for the first time in my life I stopped cooking. I couldn't face eating anything apart from a few olives, sun-dried tomatoes and custard creams. I retreated into a shell. All my family and friends were as bewildered and shocked as I was. If I had been on my own, I would never have coped. I'm distraught, completely devastated, but I don't want or need revenge,' she said. 'I may be distraught over what's happened, but I don't feel bitter or angry. That's just not me. If you have these awful, dreadful feelings of upset and anger, it just destroys you and eats you up. It hurts me that our marriage is over, but I don't want any more damage done to Paul, me or Joshua.'

In fact, Alexandra went as far to say that she hoped that her and Paul could maintain a civil relationship for the sake of their son. 'We love Joshua to bits,' she said. 'He's all right, he's a little soldier, but he's only 11 and any child going through a family crisis like this is going to be affected, so we are trying our utmost to make sure this is as civil, easy and as smooth as possible for him. Josh loves his Daddy and I wouldn't want it any other way. You have to take one day at a time. That's what I say to Joshua. Each day you do it step by step, but this is all new to me, so it's hard, but it has to be done and I know things will get better.'

Alexandra even acknowledged that her use of Twitter to help deal with the break-up was something that she regretted in hindsight. But, again, it shows something of the kind of woman she is that she was able to admit that so honestly and publicly. 'I know I shouldn't have done it and I regret it,' she told the newspaper. 'I've always said to our son: "When you are scared of something, if you laugh at it, then humour takes all the scariness out of it." That's what I tried to do, but it was wrong. I was in a very unhappy, dark place at that time.'

And despite the very public and very messy nature of her split, Alexandra said in her interview that she was trying her very best to cling on to the good times she and Paul shared during their 15 years of marriage. 'The door was always open to our house. People knew that if they came in I'd be in the kitchen and if they arrived at the right time, they'd be offered food,' said Alexandra. 'With Joshua being an only child, I wanted our house to be filled with noise, people, bustle and activity with people popping in for a glass of wine or nibbles I'd made. There's nothing nicer than having people sitting around my whopping dining table, connecting over wonderful food and breaking bread. That's what family was all about for us.'

Alexandra herself was the first to admit that their relationship, like many others, had its ups and downs. But nevertheless, she was always bowled over by the fact that Paul was so loving and caring towards her and Joshua. 'Our marriage wasn't perfect, but it was happy, normal and Paul was a wonderful husband,' she told the interviewer. 'He was so thoughtful. I remember for my fortieth birthday he surprised me by taking me to Rome, managing to keep it secret until 12 hours before we left. He was very good at choosing presents, always buying just the right thing. I'd come home from shopping and he'd have baked something special, saying: "Look, I've made you this." He really is the most brilliant baker; his Yorkshire puddings defy gravity. And he's a wonderful dad. He loves Josh to pieces. They are similar characters, almost like twins.'

Alexandra, who said she would like to now publish a cookery book, recalled how nothing seemed untoward while Paul was in America at the beginning of 2013. They talked via Skype every day and spoke twice a day on the phone, but it was not a happy reunion on his return. Instantly, Alexandra knew something was wrong. And it changed forever, never to return to normal. 'My first reaction was one of disbelief. I couldn't believe it was happening,' she said. 'I was completely devastated. I loved being in a family, but suddenly I just didn't have that option any more. I took off my wedding ring the day we decided to separate, because it felt wrong to wear it. I keep it somewhere safe, but I will never wear it again. I have spent 15 years of my life with this man, working towards this goal. He is brilliant at what he does and is passionate about baking.

That is what motivates him, not fame. When *Bake Off* returns, of course I'll watch it. My son wants to. He's incredibly proud of his Daddy, so I will watch it with him.'

It must have been a difficult moment for Paul if he read the interview, as it brought into sharp focus just how much his life had changed in such a short space of time. Meanwhile, news about his US show seemed to be going from bad to worse.

Soon after Alexandra's interview, it was reported that the ratings of *The American Baking Competition* had sunk so low that CBS had decided to pull the plug on a second series of the show, meaning it was being scrapped after just one series. Towards the end of July 2013, the *Mail On Sunday* reported that the show's staff were told to 'take alternative employment' in September instead of filming a second series. A production source was quoted as saying: 'It's over. It's been cancelled. We've all been waiting for CBS to tell us if they were going to pick us up for a second series and this week the call came in saying it's not being renewed and we should take alternative employment offers. Critics hated it and the ratings were abysmal. None of us are particularly surprised, to be honest.'

It went on to say that the series had only managed to peak at relatively meagre 5.8 million viewers, but that figure had quickly spiralled downwards as the series continued. The production source also said the rumours of an affair between Paul and his co-host had caused a viewer backlash on the internet with American viewers bombarding the CBS site with critical comments. In turn, the source claimed, this played a big part in the cancellation. Even so, Love Productions insisted in a statement that CBS were yet to decide whether or not they would definitely scrap the show. Nevertheless, it wasn't looking good.

But Paul's passion for his chosen profession would almost certainly keep him going during these difficult times. While baking had become a serious job and a stellar career for him, he has often spoken of how he indulges in food, baking and other culinary delights as a pastime – obviously he sees it as an escape. And now, as he battled through undoubtedly one of the most difficult episodes ever, he may have appreciated the finer things in life even more than before. In an interview with the *Independent* prior to the split with Alexandra, he was asked if he only had £10 to spend on food, where would he spend it and on what? Paul was categorical in his response – the whole lot would go on chocolate! 'I'd probably head straight to Paul A Young, the chocolatier,' he declared. 'Paul is a magician with flavours, using balsamic, ginger, martini everything. Otherwise, I'd head to the Loire, the medieval city of Loches, where there is a little bakery just outside the city walls. It bakes tiny, warm breads filled with cheese and smoked lardons.'

And when it came to his favourite comfort food, once again he would choose chocolate. 'Definitely my Sachertorte (chocolate again!) with a large dollop of crème fraîche on the side. It's gooey, indulgent and I'd probably eat a full one if my wife let me.'

And if there was one treat that he could choose over anything else, his 'Desert Island meal', it was the humble pork pie, although in this case it happened to be a gourmet one. 'It's got to be my pork pie recipe, made with pork loin, back bacon and lots of fresh parsley,' he enthused. 'Real pork pies are meaty and filling and should always be homemade.'

Luxury-loving Paul's favourite restaurant is Pollen Street Social in London's West End, run by world-renowned restaurateur Jason Atherton, the man behind Michelin-starred eatery Maze. 'Jason Atherton knows his stuff,' Paul told the *Independent*. 'I'd eat there every night if I could.'

No stranger to the finer things in life, Paul also detailed in an article with the *Daily Telegraph* his favourite hotels around the UK. Unsurprisingly, two of the hotels where he spent his formative years as a baker feature in the list: the Chester Grosvenor and Cliveden House are two of his favourite places to stay. Talking about the Chester Grosvenor, he mentioned – you've guessed it – the great baked products available, saying: 'For a city break, this Grade II listed hotel in the walled city of Chester is perfect. The rooms are luxurious and the restaurant is fantastic. Run by Michelin-starred chef Simon Radley, it has a beautiful orangery roof, an enormous variety of breads and one of the biggest wine cellars I've seen.' And on Cliveden House, he commented on the grand surroundings of the hotel, coupled with the top-notch food: 'A beautiful old stately home that used to be owned by Lady Astor, this hotel has everything: National Trust managed Grade I listed gardens and woodlands, a snooker room and even a boat you can have afternoon tea on. The Michelin-starred restaurant has floor-to-ceiling windows overlooking the gardens and top-quality food: perfect sauces, classic gratins, amazing pastry and legendary steaks.'

Other establishments to have similarly impressed him over the years include the luxury Somerset hotel Ston Easton Park, which was built in the eighteenth century for John Hippisley Coxe, whose family had been Lords of the Manor of Ston Easton since 1544. Paul said: 'The hotel itself is stunning – a classic gatehouse set in 60 acres – but it's the food at The Sorrel restaurant that keeps me coming back. It's based on fresh, locally sourced produce, so the menu changes regularly with the seasons. The menu is classic with a modern twist; their passion fruit roulade is to die for.'

Next on his list was The Timber Batts Inn, Kent – relatively near to his former marital home. Paul said: 'This cosy fifteenth-century village inn is run by a classically trained French chef, which might explain why the restaurant, Froggies, is always full. Absolutely everything is made in house, from the parfaits to the pâté to the breads, and they're all spectacular. The wine list is extensive, they serve lovely local ales and the rooms are comfortable, clean and reasonably priced.' Another Kent hotel that Paul pinpointed as being one of his favourites was the Rocksalt in Folkestone. He said: 'This is a relatively new but very cool place specialising in unbelievably fresh fish. They serve great lobster and langoustines, have their own fish smokery and the kitchen is glass-fronted so you can watch the chefs. The rooms are modern and chic.'

And while he may well be partial to posh eateries and high-end hotels, Paul is just as happy to enjoy cooking at home. In fact, he often sees it as a more enjoyable experience than splashing out on an expensive meal. Ultimately, though, his first love remains baking. He says it's partly because anyone can get involved in it. 'One of the reasons is because baking is more approachable [than other types of cooking] at any level,' he told the *Daily Telegraph*. 'So, whether you're making a pie, a pasty, a sponge cake, a cupcake, a muffin ... if you've got a set of scales, good ingredients, a good recipe, anyone – from the age of eight to 80 – can do it.'

While his skills may have taken years to perfect, he insists that baking can be very straightforward, so long as you're patient enough to follow a recipe. 'A sponge is quite simple,' he told the *Daily Telegraph*. 'You weigh ingredients, mix and put it in the oven. With pastry you manhandle it, shape it, fold it. You have to be involved with it, there is more jeopardy, more risk. But it's like making a casserole. There's a flurry of activity to begin with then it's about leaving it to rest.'

For anyone wishing to get into baking, he recommends a pain au chocolat as a good 'first pastry', adding: 'You could do a couple of batches of croissant dough, date it, put it in the freezer and in half a morning's work you have two months' worth of croissants.' But he insists that it's important not to get frustrated if your cake doesn't rise or your croissants end up soggy. He admits that despite his tough-talking judging on *The Great British Bake Off*, he too sometimes struggles to meet his own impeccably high standards. 'Even I don't always come up to my own standards of perfection,' he told the *Daily Telegraph*.

But when it comes to what he personally would like to whip up when he has a spare hour or two on his hands, alpha-male Paul is adamant that it's fairy cakes. 'It's not good for my image, but I like baking fairy cakes,' he told the *Sunday Express*. 'It's not very macho but my son loves them.'

In the same interview he admitted that his passion for baking means that he can never walk past a bakery without going in. 'I have to go in and check it out, whether I'm home or abroad,' he said. 'I'll always buy something to taste.'

And despite all the fancy kit that is used on *The Great British Bake Off*, Paul claims the only essential is a set of digital scales. 'Everything else is luxury,' he told the *Daily Telegraph*. 'Consistency in measurements is key. Don't change your ingredients or you'll end up blaming the recipe.' Even so, he admits that he has indulged in a few more 'luxury' items that help him create the perfect bakes. His most used piece of kitchen kit is his KitchenAid, an electronic mixer. He told the *Independent*: 'I love all the accessories, in particular the dough hook. It's very similar to the big industrial-size mixer I have in the bakery and I use it whenever I bake at home.' Meanwhile, his least favourite item is the microwave – no doubt because he never has a ready meal! 'I can't see the point.'

Paul's favourite cookbook is *A History of Food in 100 Recipes* by William Sitwell because 'it's everything I'm passionate about: history, baking and food. A great read.'

With his love of hearty food and baking, one journalist thought it might be interesting to ask what Paul would choose if he could only eat bread or potatoes for the rest of his life. He was adamant that it would be bread. 'Obviously bread,' was his response. 'I do love roast potatoes, dauphinoise, even plain boiled the way my nan used to make them but bread is the basis of a good meal. I lived in Cyprus for many years and travelled through the Middle East so I learnt that you can stuff a pitta with salads, meats and herbs and have the freshest, tastiest meal ever. I love the way the Italians use their stale bread up as well, as bruschetta or covered in crushed garlic and olive oil, torn into pieces and tossed in a salad with capers, anchovies, onion and crisp lettuce.'

With such a fierce passion and commitment to baking, it's no wonder Paul would emerge as one of Britain's favourite people to bake with according to research by the Cake Awards, while his *Great British Bake Off* co-judge Mary Berry was the person most people in the UK would like to bake with (more than half of all the respondents). In second place, with a sizeable 15 per cent of the votes, domestic goddess Nigella Lawson was also a firm favourite. Interestingly, many of the voters saw their grans or their mums as their best baking companions. Meanwhile, many of the participants said they enjoyed baking because it helped relieve stress and enhances relaxation. Others baked cakes because they want to know what is in the food they are eating, and because their children enjoy baking.

As far as Paul was concerned, it was no bad thing that so many people were taking up baking, thanks to his influence. Scores of wannabe bakers were taking to the ovens, thanks to Paul's work on shows such as *The Great British Bake Off* and *Paul Hollywood's Bread*, and because of his books, five of which he had published by 2013. He himself has said that the huge number of people who are now taking up baking holds the key to a more important issue, though. Both he and his co-presenter Mary Berry believe compulsory lessons in home economics – where students are taught how to cook for themselves – would help tackle Britain's obesity crisis. 'It needs to be put back on [the curriculum] so that people have a basic understanding of what we're eating. It makes a huge difference,' he told the *Sun*'s Sunday edition in a joint interview with Mary. She agreed, saying it was particularly important 'as the country is obese'.

In Britain, home economics is still taught as part of Key Stage 3 Design & Technology for 11 to 14 year olds, but these two TV chefs feel that it should be taught more widely. What's more, Paul and Mary are not the only ones who agree that teaching kids from a young age how to cook would help tackle the obesity crisis. Fellow TV chef Jamie Oliver formally wrote to Prime Minister David Cameron asking him to introduce a minimum of 24 hours a year of practical cooking lessons and food education for pupils aged four to 14.

And childhood obesity really has become a major issue in the UK over the last few years. According to the Association for the Study of Obesity, it is a 'serious problem', while the Organisation for Economic Co-operation and Development (OECD) said earlier in 2013 that adult obesity rates in the UK are significantly higher than the average in most of the developed world. According to the statistics, 24 per cent of women and 22 per cent of men are now obese, whereas in other parts of the world the average is approximately 17 per cent.

And as far as Paul was concerned, baking – and home cooking more specifically – was something that would help to bring this escalating problem under control. Not only was it something to be enjoyed and relished, but an important skill that can change the way we live our lives for the better.

It was unquestionable that Paul Hollywood had become a hugely influential figure in British cooking. But what would the future hold for him? There were more series of *The Great British Bake Off* in the pipeline and doubtless still more solo projects would be offered him, given that the BBC had issued a statement confirming their intentions to work with Paul in the future. More books would be planned, and regardless of what had happened in his private life, his star would continue to rise.

Non-cookery related shows would also come knocking. In June 2013 it appeared that Paul was on his way to securing a role on one of Britain's biggest reality TV shows, *Strictly Come Dancing*. The ballroom dance competition was one of the country's most popular shows and had even managed to edge ahead of its closest rival, ITV's *X Factor*, in the 2012 ratings. And now the much-loved series, which saw celebrities partnered with professional ballroom and Latin dancers as they competed to lift the coveted glitterball trophy, appeared to have its sights set on Paul. And why not? It seemed liked a smart move on the BBC's part. After all, he already appealed to their core female viewership – even if this popularity may have been ever so slightly diminished owing to his separation from Alexandra – and it would be exciting to see how he performed outside of the kitchen.

Reports began to circulate that BBC bosses were after him, first in the *Sunday People*, which wrote: 'Hunky Paul is cooking up a lucrative move to *Strictly Come Dancing*, the

BBC has revealed. BBC bosses want the *Great British Bake Off* host to join their ballroom hit when it kicks off again this autumn'. The story quoted a source 'close to Paul': '*Strictly* are desperate to get him on the show and the BBC think it will be a really good move. Paul has been telling his friends how keen he is to get involved. He watches it all the time and wanted to go on it last year. He has had a lot on his mind and is throwing himself into different projects.'

Obviously with his schedule as busy as it had been in recent months, it would depend on whether or not Paul would have the time to do the show. The source went on to say: 'It depends on schedules. He is busy filming *Bake Off*, which starts in August, and is keen to sign on the dotted line. The Beeb are constantly looking at ways to step up the war with ITV over primetime Saturday-night viewing. They know what a hit he is with viewers and think he will go far in the competition.' Other stars being considered for the 2013 series included the *Coronation Street* actress Natalie Gumede as well as former *X Factor* winner-turned-opera-singer Joe McElderry.

And it seemed Paul was game for something new. 'I'm working on some top-secret shows,' he told the *Sun* in July. 'I'm doing a show on puddings and pies. It's a more blokey show. I love the idea of puddings and pies. I love eating things like that – as you can probably tell!'

Paul made no secret of the fact that he would be extremely open to the possibility of taking on a fresh challenge like *Strictly Come Dancing*. Doubtless he would have sounded out his close friend James Martin, a previous participant in the series, to see whether or not he thought it was a good idea.

James had performed well in the competition so there's a strong chance that he may have encouraged his friend to go for it.

Talking more generally about being given the opportunity to try things outside of baking and the kitchen, Paul was quoted in the *Sunday Mirror* as saying: 'It's all about timing. When you become a product of a big programme, you get busier and it's hard trying to fit everything in. I am just really enjoying myself.' Previously, on the subject of *Strictly*, he quite categorically said that he would be willing to sign up for the show. He told the *Daily Mail* in 2013: 'I wouldn't mind doing *Strictly* this year.' On top of that, he sounded pretty confident about his chances. 'My wife Alexandra says I was the only person she'd ever danced with who she wasn't embarrassed to be with, so I take that as a good sign,' he continued. 'I was dancing recently. There was me, my wife, James, Olly Smith and their partners at a charity thing for children with cancer. James has done *Strictly*, so I thought I'd steal a few moves but he was just doing this kind of *Stomp* thing. I thought, I could do that.' Later, other reports would surface that would suggest that he was weighing up whether or not to sign up for the series on account of his looming divorce from Alexandra and the fact he wanted to spend as much time as possible with Joshua when he wasn't involved in his various other projects.

And so whether he would sign on the dotted line and throw himself into the ballroom competition remains to be seen. But what was clear was that he was now a veritable star in the UK. From humble beginnings in the Wirral to his position as one of the country's foremost master bakers, two qualities had allowed him to reach the top of his profession: hard graft and undeniable passion for everything he did. Whatever his next move would be, Paul Hollywood was destined to continue on a stellar trajectory. His path to the top had undeniably not been an easy one; he had had to make sacrifices to carve out his position as the best in the business. Meanwhile, his seemingly perfect family life had taken a battering after his stardom went through the roof. No matter what happened next in his personal life or career, though, there was one thing that he could rely on – the fact that his legions of fans around the world were waiting with baited breath to see what he would do next, and whatever path he chose to take, they would be there to support him.

He is, after all, Britain's best-loved baker.

# CHAPTER 16

# The Future

But it didn't end there. Like any good episode of the *Bake Off*, Paul's life continued to take a series of unexpected twists and turns. With all the ups and downs he had experienced in his personal life, he would inevitably have been on the lookout for some good news elsewhere in his life. And while by the summer of 2013 a new series of the *Bake Off* was in the process of being filmed, it seemed the possibility of returning to America to continue working on TV there was fading – and fast.

After a lukewarm response from audiences and critics in the US, the chances of *The American Baking Competition* being renewed – and Paul continuing to build his profile stateside – were on a knife-edge. It was becoming clear that bosses at CBS were unhappy with the response the programme had been generating. While *Bake Off* had become one c f British TV's biggest shows, its US counterpart was fail:ng to create anywhere near enough hype. It's often said that in America the TV business is more ruthless than anywhere else in the world, and Paul was about to experience that first-hand.

In July 2013 it was revealed that *The American Baking Competition* would not be brought back for another series. The *Mail on Sunday*'s LA correspondent reported that the programme's producers had been advised by network executives to 'take alternative employment' in September, rather than expect to return to work on a second series of the show. The paper also quoted a 'production source' who said: 'We've all been waiting for CBS to tell us if they were going to pick us up for a second series and this week the call came in saying it's not being renewed and we should take alternative employment offers.' The source added: 'None of us are particularly surprised, to be honest.'

It was a sad ending to a venture that for Paul appeared to have so much promise to begin with. For the time being he remained quiet about the demise of *The American Baking Competition* and his spokespeople politely declined to comment on the news of the cancellation. But it would have been a bitter blow after committing so much time and energy to the show. Anyone in his position would have been disappointed.

So, with his tail between his legs, he came back to the UK, where it was a case of returning to the familiar. The fourth series of the *Bake Off* was on TV screens in August, with all the usual fanfare and excitement. It seemed that, irrespective of what had happened in the US and with Paul's private life, the British public still adored the show that had first made him a star.

The eventual winner would be Frances Quinn, a designer who had previously worked at companies in London and Vancouver. However, the story of the series was Paul's interaction with another contestant – philosophy and history student Ruby Tandoh, who was 21 years old at the time of the series airing.

Ruby was originally from Essex and had, for a short time, been signed up to the modelling agency Models 1 before starting her degree at University College London. During the course of filming, she was juggling studying for exams and preparing for the show's tough weekly tasks, something that was often referenced during the course of the programme. Very early on in the series, however, there were suggestions that Paul was enjoying a flirtatious rapport with Ruby and some even went so far as to suggest that he was showing her favouritism. It was too good a story for the national newspapers to ignore – Paul, who had just come out of a 15-year marriage after an affair, was now showing signs of being 'sweet' on one of his show's contestants, as one tabloid journalist put it. The *Daily Mail* reported that 'Casanova Paul Hollywood is spicing up *The Great British Bake Off* once again, with fans pointing to simmering sexual tension between him and contestant Ruby Tandoh'.

Viewers on Twitter were also quick to jump on the banter between Paul and Ruby – although it's safe to say there was never anything more than a strictly professional judge-contestant relationship between the pair. Both were adamant that there was no such flirtatious behaviour between them and Paul even said that Ruby's fellow competitor Kimberley Wilson was 'much prettier'.

It was later, in 2015, when it became clear that any suggestion of unprofessionalism between the two was widely off the mark. Posting a video of the Diana Ross song 'I'm Coming Out', Ruby proudly announced on Twitter that she was a lesbian, revealing she had told her parents her news and that she felt 'free' after doing so. She also used the opportunity to take a swipe at anyone who had ever suggested that she had flirted with Paul to get ahead in the *Bake Off*. Speaking quite forthrightly about it, she tweeted: 'p.s. for those who thought I fancied Paul Hollywood or that I'd ever bang him to get ahead – JOKE'S ON YOU, YOU MASSIVE S****ING MISOGYNISTS.' Off the back of the fame she achieved by appearing on the *Bake Off*, Ruby would go on to write regularly about baking for the *Guardian* newspaper (pointedly, she wrote in one column, 'I'd rather eat my own foot than attempt to seduce my way to victory').

Back in 2013, the fourth series was over. It was considered another triumph, with ratings once again on the up and confirmation that it would return again for another outing the following year quick to follow. But a short while after the finale, Paul's private life once again returned to the pages of the national newspapers. Nothing to do with Ruby this time – now it seemed there was a chance that he and his wife Alexandra might get back together. Despite her insistence that she would get a divorce following Paul's infidelity, rumours had started to swirl that the pair were meeting up again. It seemed like yet another unexpected twist in the Paul Hollywood story. Alexandra had appeared so adamant that her marriage was well and truly over in an interview she gave to the *Daily Mail* and, simultaneously, so focused on making life as a single mother work, that no one could have predicted that she would have such a change of heart.

In November 2013, the *Daily Mail* reported that the estranged couple had been enjoying 'date nights' at the homes they were renting in Kent. The journalist who wrote the article said that Alex had taken some much-needed 'thinking time' during the recent half term and had flown off to the south of France with a group of girlfriends. It can only be assumed what she was 'thinking' about was whether or not to give her husband a second chance. The article suggested she was being counselled by her sister. Meanwhile, it was also reported that Mary Berry had stayed in touch with Alexandra during the whole ordeal and was 'willing' the couple to give their marriage another go.

Set alongside this, it appeared that Paul's relationship with Marcela Valladolid had gone sour. Whether the spark had gone, or if there had been a falling out or they had just drifted apart, it wasn't initially clear. However, when Paul gave an interview, speaking about the demise of *The American Baking Competition*, it certainly seemed like there was no love lost between them. Talking to Valentine Lowe from *The Times*, he suggested that he and Marcela had been incompatible when it came to their relationship on screen and that was the reason why the programme had not gone down well with the viewing public. He claimed that if he had been cast alongside someone more like Mary Berry then the series might have fared better. 'We were looking at another woman who was more like [fellow judge] Mary [Berry],' he told *The Times*. 'I think that dynamic worked. I think you want expertise, experience. I just think Marcela was slightly too young, that's all. It came down to experience. And she's more known for enchiladas, Mexican food, not for baking.' There was also some suggestion that, despite *The American Baking Competition* falling flat on CBS, rival networks were looking at taking the format and trying to bring back the series, albeit with some tweaks to make sure it didn't hit a bum note again. Whether this would come to fruition, only time would tell but it appeared clear from Paul's comments that he wouldn't be reunited with Marcela either on or off screen.

Whatever had happened to bring an end to his relationship with Marcela, Paul seemed to realise that he had made a terrible mistake in throwing away his marriage to Alexandra. Now he wanted to make amends, and he was happy to tell the world about it in the most public way possible. In an interview with Radio 5 Live, Paul appeared to wear his heart on his sleeve – not only confessing to his affair, but also insisting that he wanted to win Alexandra back. During his appearance on the show, he said: 'I did have an affair in America with my co-judge and it was something which was the biggest mistake of my life because, actually, I still love my wife.'

He went so far as to reveal that he and Alexandra were working things through but admitted that he was still a long way off from totally convincing her reconciliation was the right thing. He told Richard Bacon: 'I'm at that point at the moment where we're talking and we're working to get back together again. But it is going to take time.'

Paul appeared acutely aware that he had also put his reputation as one of Britain's best-loved celebrities in jeopardy too – but he took full responsibility for bringing it on himself. Speaking about the furious backlash from fans and the media, he told Radio 5 Live: 'It was deserved because what I did was wrong. I've taken it. It was my punishment. At the end of the day we're moving on and I'm in a much better place. I'm getting emotional now.'

It all appeared too much for Paul but if Alexandra wanted a sign that he was sorry, there was no grander gesture than going on national radio and admitting he was totally in the wrong.

Paul didn't stop there, however. He seemed insistent on going all out to make sure that the public and, above all, Alexandra, knew that he regretted ever cheating on her. Just days after appearing on Radio 5 Live, he then appeared on *The Jonathan Ross Show* on ITV. Described as 'grim-faced' and 'grovelling' by the *Daily Mail*, he said: 'I made the biggest mistake of my life and I regret it. At the moment, Alex and I are working things through together. We're just going to take things one step at a time, but I still love her and that's ultimately what it is.'

He was also clear that his indiscretions had made life difficult, not just for him and Alexandra, but his son Josh, too. He told Valentine Lowe of *The Times*: 'My boy and me are very close. He's hurt. I was hurt when I was a kid. I know what it's like, more so than anybody.' In the same article he admitted that the speculation, pressure and fall-out from his affair with Marcela had been tortuous for him personally, too. When asked if it had all got too much and if he had 'succumbed to the pressure', he replied: 'Yes, certainly the last few months I have. Now, I'm out of the woods. I see it for what it is now and what it was.' When asked whether the constant criticism over his actions from the media had got to him, he replied: 'You have no idea. They got to me. I won't forget that, but revenge is a dish best served cold. I'm a Scouser at the end of the day. I was hurt. I was hurt.'

By the end of the year, Paul's efforts to convince Alexandra that he was truly and genuinely sorry had paid off. After all his grovelling, both in person and on TV and radio, it seemed she had, finally, forgiven him. The family flew off together to enjoy a Christmas skiing holiday in the French Alps. Their decision to spend Christmas away from Kent was possibly influenced by the difficult year they had all had and a desire just to get away from it all. Whatever the case, things were clearly back on track. On Boxing Day, the couple confirmed they were fully reconciled and loved up once again when Alexandra posted a photo of them toasting each other with a glass of bubbly on the social media site Instagram. Scores of Alexandra's followers appeared delighted by the news, posting their congratulations under the photo. The pair couldn't have looked happier and there was no indication of the difficult periods they had experienced that year. Some said they even looked as though they had never had so much as a blip in their relationship. Alongside the happy snap, Alexandra included the words: 'Happy Christmas All!' For the Hollywoods, it certainly was.

But many people had seen the reconciliation coming. In the weeks leading up to the couple's romantic French getaway, Alexandra had once again been spotted out and about wearing her diamond ring on her wedding finger. Newspaper photographers had also caught the pair sharing kisses after date nights out, which had become increasingly frequent following Paul's public declarations that he wanted to make amends for his mistakes. After returning from France, the family were then seen out shopping in the January sales, enjoying getting their hands on as many bargains as possible and indulging in some quality time before 2014 got into full swing.

It was a total change of heart for Alexandra, who had previously given a newspaper interview to the *Daily Mail* insisting there was no going back after Paul's indiscretions. 'I love my husband and I was, and still am very proud of what he has achieved, but there is no going back and I just want this finished with and to move on,' she told Helen Weathers from the newspaper at the time. She continued: 'In the space of four weeks my life changed irrevocably. One minute I was happily married and the next I wasn't. It was a complete shock. I still haven't completely absorbed it yet. Sometimes I wake up in the morning and can't believe it's happened. I feel utterly bewildered and incredibly sad. Paul went to America and when he came back everything was different, everything had changed.'

Now it seemed everything had changed again – but for the better, with the couple fully back on track. Doubtless the decision to trust Paul and let him back into her life must have taken a lot of soul-searching and sleepless nights but after 15 years of marriage, and having brought up a child together, Alexandra obviously thought their relationship was worth fighting for.

If anything, the interim period where Alexandra went from being happily married to a single mum before getting back together again with Paul would have made her a stronger person. It was plain to see from social media accounts like Twitter that she had built up her own fan base who supported her during those difficult times and kept her going. Her fans also enjoyed the fact that she would often take to Twitter to post photographs of food she had cooked that day for herself, Josh and her friends. Paul had always said that Alexandra excelled in the kitchen – not just with baking, but cooking generally. Her followers on Twitter were now treated to an endless stream of stews, salads, breakfasts, curries and dishes from all round the world as it appeared Alexandra cooked her way through her heartbreak. 'I used to tweet if repeats of *Bake Off* were on or when Paul was away filming. It wasn't about me but it was about our family life, which was intrinsic to Paul's career,' she said in an interview with Elizabeth Sanderson from the *Mail on Sunday*. 'And then, of course, everything happened and I stopped tweeting. Then a friend from Cyprus tweeted, "chin up" and loads of other people followed. I looked at all these messages people had sent. I was amazed that people I didn't know could be so kind and supportive.'

She would post the snaps on an almost daily basis – and whether or not she intended it, it seemed her photos would become the start of a new career for Alexandra. With her personal profile higher than ever (albeit thanks to Paul's affair), cookbook publishers and TV cookery show producers started to consider Alex as an option to become a new celebrity chef. Her appeal was obvious – a normal mum who had cooked all her life and whom the public now felt increasingly affectionate towards after everything she had been through.

Suddenly Alex was inundated with offers. Not the kind she was used to – to give tell-all interviews about her anguish over her marriage – but to cook. Indeed, the offers came in so thick and fast that she was forced to employ a well-known agent to field them all. Suddenly there was talk of books and TV shows of her own – it was all happening rather quickly.

After the Christmas holiday in the Alps, the first of these offers would see the light of day. In January 2014, Alexandra was signed up to launch her own cookery segment on the hit daytime TV show *Lorraine* on ITV. Fronted by the much-loved presenter Lorraine Kelly, the programme had, for a long time, featured a cookery slot. In recent years, it had been presented by a roster of well-known chefs, including the *MasterChef* 2005 winner Dean Edwards, restaurateur James Tanner and the series three *Bake Off* winner, John Whaite. Now, Alexandra would be joining the line-up.

The first dish that she would cook would be a 'sinless southern baked chicken', which she said she picked because it was easy to whip up after a hard day at work or following the school run, and it was tasty but not unhealthy either. It was a dish, Alexandra said, that 'brought the whole family together' whenever she would cook it at home. As the segment went on, the audience clearly loved her and took to Twitter to say how natural and experienced she seemed, despite it being her first ever go at being on TV.

If Alexandra had been nervous it didn't show – and that may have been because she had support in the wings as she brought Paul along with her. To the surprise of everyone, he watched from the sidelines as Alex chatted and cooked on the programme, willing her on to do the best job possible. After a tough few months, the fact that he had accompanied her to the set at the London Studios on such an important day for her was concrete proof the pair were closer than ever. When Alexandra's chicken dish was ready to be taste-tested, he even agreed to come onto the set and try the dish and offer words of support live on air. Speaking to Lorraine about the encouragement Paul had given her, Alexandra said: 'He's hugely supportive. In fact, he's here today, he's here to come and hold my hand because it's my first live TV appearance so, yes, it's going well.'

Alexandra was also open about how difficult the process of reconciling had been over the previous few months, speaking candidly to Lorraine about the pressure she and the family had been under in a sofa interview before she was unleashed on the kitchen. 'Things are good, actually,' she told Lorraine. 'I had a wonderful Christmas, a wonderful family Christmas – we really enjoyed it. It has been a tough year, it's really hard when you have your life splashed all over the papers but you've got to get on with it, haven't you? You've got to get on with it and make the best of what it is and you know, hey, I'm sitting here.'

She also spoke about her love of cooking and the fact that it ran in the family. Not only had she and Paul cooked together over the years, but she had learnt from her mum and grandmothers too. 'It's in the blood! I'm a cook, I'm not a chef,' she said. 'I never would set myself up to be a chef but my great grandmother was actually like Mrs Patmore in *Downton Abbey*... she was a fabulous cook as well, she lived in France and she made films over there with my grandfather, who was a film producer over there, but she was a prodigious cook, and then of course my mother who I get most of my influence from, she's an incredible cook as well so from a very early age I've been cooking. I think the earliest I can remember is four years old, standing on a stool in the kitchen.'

Meanwhile, Paul looked on, prouder than ever of everything that his wife was achieving. Despite all that had happened, it was clear that she had a new-found independence and while she would go on to become a regular on *Lorraine* after such a successful debut, her TV gig wouldn't be the only high-profile project that she would be involved in over the coming months. She hinted on the programme that there was a cookbook in the offing too. 'I'm really excited about being here today, really, really excited. I've got loads of things in the pipeline... so it's not all bad,' she said. 'I'm really excited about the whole thing, like I said, I've got a book on the boil at the moment.'

The book would end up being published in February 2015 and Alexandra called it *My Busy Kitchen – A Lifetime of Family Recipes*. Fittingly, the dedication at the front of the book says 'For Mumma' – in tribute to the fact that she learned all the recipes from her family. Those recipes included quick mid-week meals, salads, breakfasts and dinners that could be easily rustled up even if you didn't have much time. Critics heaped praise on the book, which went on to sell well. Doubtless similar projects would be in the pipeline for Alexandra in the future too, after the success of the book and her segment on *Lorraine*.

But most importantly, developing her own cookery career seemed to give Alexandra a new lease of life. For years she had loyally supported Paul as his career went from strength to strength. Now this was the opportunity for Alexandra to show the world exactly what she could do and showcase her own talents. Understandably it was something she found nerve-wracking, but also liberating. 'Before, I was behind the scenes – very active but still in the background – so it's strange for me to push myself forwards,' she said in an interview with the *Mail on Sunday*. 'It's not about finding it liberating, I just think I need to do it.'

So with his marriage back on track and Paul prouder than ever of everything his wife was achieving, you might imagine that he was hoping life would quieten down for a bit. Another new series of the *Bake Off* was set to film in the summer of 2014, and in the meantime he was beginning a nationwide tour with his newly devised show, *Get Your Bake On*. It would see Paul teach fans how to make their favourite recipes during a live show, and the audience would even get the chance to meet the man himself afterwards. Tickets sold out swiftly as the tour, which initially included 23 dates around the country, was so successful that it was decided that it would return with another 27 dates in the autumn, around the same time that the *Bake Off* was back on air. After the blip of his affair, Paul's popularity was greater than ever.

However, as seemed to be becoming the norm, there was yet another twist coming for Paul. In May 2014, reports surfaced in the *Daily Telegraph* that his artisan bread company was struggling to turn a profit. According to them the company accounts of the firm, The Paul Hollywood Artisan Bread LLP, were in the red. The paper reported that they owed close to £60,000, with £28,616 of that figure owed directly to Paul himself. And it wasn't the first time that the sums had not added up. The *Daily Telegraph* went on to say in its report that the firm had also sunk £11,793 into the red in the financial year up until 30 June 2012. Enough was enough, and the business was wound up – although Paul said that it was mainly owing to the fact that his TV work meant he wasn't able to focus his attention fully on the company 'It's a huge headache and massive problem because I wasn't there enough,' the *Daily Telegraph* article quoted him as saying.

Unfortunately for Paul, it wasn't the first time that he had had to shut down one of his businesses. According to the paper, in 2003 he also liquidated his firm Hollywood Bread, which posted debts of £262,000 according to papers that totted up the sums for when it was closed, around Christmas 2005.

That said it was fair to assume that despite those businesses being wound up, Paul was making a mint. With his TV work, books and tours, it's safe to say he was bringing home the bacon. His other company, Paul Hollywood Limited, which looked after his other business interests, wasn't tarnished by the bread businesses going under. Indeed, far from it. In fact it was reported to be making a very healthy turnover, at one stage posting a £409,730 profit, according to the same report in the *Daily Telegraph*.

And the money didn't stop coming in. Later in 2014, there were suggestions that Paul had truly hit the big time – and made a cool £1 million. It can only be an estimate, however the *Daily Mail* tried to quantify exactly what the figure comprised of. It suggested that he had banked £300,000 for his TV work. Not only did this include his payment for the *Bake Off*, but also for his two spin-off shows – *Paul Hollywood's Bread* and *Paul Hollywood's Pies & Puds*. On top of that, the paper said that he would have made another £300,000 from his three best-selling books, with each of them being 'released to coincide with his television projects', adding that: '*Pies & Puds*, which tied in with his 20-part BBC2 series, came second in the Christmas bestsellers list and has sold more than 100,000 to date.' By anyone's standards, those sales figures were exceptionally good. The paper then suggested he could have made anywhere between £20,000 and £50,000 for a string of merchandise which he had started selling via his own website. Items that his adoring fans could get their hands on included T-shirts and hoodies with his 'Get Your Bake On' slogan from his live shows across the front, along with a whole range of branded spoons, tea towels and bags. If you wanted a tour programme with that extra-special twist – Paul's autograph – that was also available for the princely sum of £13. The tour itself, the paper said, made him another £300,000. Brand Paul Hollywood was stronger than ever.

To top that success, when the *Bake Off* returned in 2014, the show also enjoyed renewed success. The ratings simply grew and grew until, incredibly, the series managed to get more viewers for one episode than the World Cup Final, which was held that year in Rio de Janeiro. This, in turn, led to speculation that the programme's judges and presenters were in line for a bumper pay rise to reflect their popularity. Meanwhile, another 6 million people would also tune into *The Great Comic Relief Bake Off* in 2015 – a version of the show featuring a string of celebrities, including the fashion expert Gok Wan and model and *Strictly* 2013 champion Abbey Clancy, all with the aim of raising money for good causes.

And during an appearance on *Desert Island Discs* in March 2015, Paul revealed one particular anecdote that acknowledged just how big a hit *Bake Off* had become. After they had finished filming one particular episode Mary Berry had offered to do his ironing for him. 'She says: "Do you need any ironing doing?" and I say, "No, I'm fine, Mary,"' he revealed on the Radio 4 programme. 'Mary Berry has ironed a few of my shirts in the first series but she doesn't now as we have wardrobe, we've gone upmarket.'

Suddenly the most menial of tasks was being taken care of for the on-screen talent!

During the interview with presenter Kirsty Young, Paul revealed the closeness that he and Mary were enjoying – perhaps, in part, because of all of the support she had given him during the more testing times over the previous couple of years. 'I drive her everywhere,' he told *Desert Island Discs*. 'Normally, when we leave the tent, she has a cold Chardonnay. So we sit outside and I either have a Hendricks or a G&T. We just sit outside and put the world to rights. Then we have dinner together and then about 9.30pm, we disappear up to bed. She is like my mother. She acts like my mother and I do treat her like my mum. She's met my mum and they get on really well. I do genuinely love Mary.'

After a difficult time during 2013, it seemed like life was back on track for Paul. He was once again focusing his attentions on making the *Bake Off* bigger and better every year – and spreading his love of baking.

'I just enjoy doing what I do,' he told Radio 4, 'And try and evangelise that through television to get people to bake.'